Claire Shaeffer's
Sewing S.O.S.

Copyright 1988 by Claire Shaeffer
Published in Menlo Park, CA, by Open Chain Publishing
Library of Congress Catalog Card Number 88-092645
ISBN 0-932086-04-7 hardbound
ISBN 0-932086-05-5 softbound
All rights reserved.
Printed in the United States of America.

Designed by Martha Vercoutere
Illustrations by Pamela S. Poole
Edited by Nancy Brazil, Marilyn Green, and Robbie Fanning
Computer aid by Tony Fanning
Cover photo by Larry Brazil

Table of Contents and Index

Add-and-fit method, 8
Ahles, Carol, 65
Alterations, 1-2, 11, 15
  bodice, 9
  business, 13
  for rounded back, 76
  pants, 68
  shoulder pads, 94
  sleeve cap, 102
  sleeves, 97
  with sloper, 73
American Home Sewing
  Association, 14
Appliqué, 2-3, 92
Apprenticeship, 12
Armhole seam, 88
Asbestos, 4
Back, rounded, 76
Balenciaga, 49, 77
Bands, 13
Batting, 4
Beads, 90
Belling side seams, 35
Belts & Buckles, 5
Bias, 6
  for piping, 78
  spaghetti straps, 103
Bias binding
  See Bindings
Bias tie collar, 21
Bindings, 6-7
Blazer interfacing, 53
Blind hemmers, 47
Blouse
  adding darts, 8
  fade line, 40
  repair, 86
  sleeve cap, 102
  sleeve ease, 99
Bodice, 8-11
Boiled wool, 39
Books, 1, 11-12
  on costume design, 21
  on designing, 75
  on grading, 71
  on tambour embroidery, 30
  tailoring, 61
Border prints, 31
Braiding foot, 78
Breaks on pants, 48
Bridal gown, 113
Bridal shop
  See Weddings
Brown, Gail, 82
Bubbling
  fusible interfacing, 57
Buckles
  See Belts & Buckles

Bumps, collar band, 19
Burda patterns, 74
Business
  home, 2, 12-13, 15
Bust darts, 8
Buttonholes, 15-17
Buttons, 17
  Chinese ball, 18
  metal, 18
Casings
  elastic, 25
  waistband, 28
Checking fit, 72
China grass, 31
China silk, 33
Clarify
  See entire book
Coat
  remodeling, 86
  Ultrasuede, 109
Coffin, David, 82
Collar band, 19
  buttonhole, 16
Collars, 19-21
  bias tie, 21
  corners, 20
  double miter, 20
  fur, 86
  interfacing, 55
Comforter, 85
Cooperative Extension Ser-
  vices, 2
Copying ready-to-wear, 70
Corded piping, 78
Corduroy
  interfacing, 53
Corners
  mitering, 64
  on piping, 80
Costume design, 21
Costume Institute, 108
Costumes, 13, 21-22
  skating, 91
Cotton fabrics
  fusible interfacing, 52
Cotton knits, 37
Cotton/poly
  pilling, 31
  sleeve ease in, 97
Cowan, Francis, 115
Creases, 22
Crepe de chine
  polyester, 53
Crepe de chine skirt, 35
Crimp, 82
Crimped hems, 50
Crochet hook embroidery,
30

Crotch
  lowering seamline, 68
Curling on knits, 37
Curves, shirttail, 82
Custom patterns, 62
Custom sewing
  See Dressmaking
Darts
  adding, 8
  bust, 9
  gaposis, 10
  on lace, 60
Denim hems, 44
Design
  costume, 21
  flat-pattern, 75
Designing, 62
Designs
  outlining, 92
Dictionary, sewing, 11
Dieting, 1
  grading patterns, 71
Dior, 49
Dodson, Jackie, 65
Double miter, 20
Drafting patterns, 62
Draperies, 38
Drawstring elastic, 24
Dress, elastic waist, 25
Dressmakers, 11, 35
Dressmaking, 2, 14
"dropped derriere", 68
Drum-and-bugle corps, 13
Ease, 42
  on hems, 50
  sleeve, 23, 97
Ease-basting, 50, 98
Elastic
  distributing fullness, 25
  drawstring, 24
  in waistbands, 26
  invisible, 23
  multiple rows, 28
  non-grow, 23
  sliding into waistbands, 28
  that grows, 27
  topstitching, 27
Elnapress®, 84
Embroidery, 30
Fabric director, 13
Fabric glue, 90
Fabric store
  starting a, 13
Fabrics
  boiled wool, 39
  breathable polyester, 39
  cotton-blend, 22
  cotton/poly blends, 31

design of, 33
foam-backed loopy, 38
fusible interfacing, 52
knit, 37
knits, 15
layout, 34
off-grain, 36
old cotton, 35
ramie, 31
sequinned, 93
sources, 37
spandex, 38
Fade line, 22, 40
Fanning, Robbie, 85
Fashion Institute of Technology, 108
Fit, 8-9, 14-15
    checking, 41, 72
    gaposis, 9
    guidelines, 41
    pants, 67
    perfect, 40
Flags, 13
Fraying, 42, 88
French handsewing, 65
Fuse-basting, 52
Fusibles
    See Interfacing, fusible
Gabardine pants, 68
Gaposis, 9
Garment
    interfaced areas, 51
Garment bags, 116
Gathering hems, 50
Glore Valcana, 110
Glue, 90
Gorge line, ripped, 61
Grading, 62, 71
Guilt
    See Fit
Hazen, Gale, 45
Hems
    by blind-hemmer, 47
    cotton knit, 38
    crimp, 50
    hand-rolled, 46
    jeans, 44
    machine-rolled, 49-50
    men's pants, 48
    narrow for wedding
        dresses, 115
    narrow pre-pleated, 49
    on collars, 20
    on pants, 47
    pleats, 44
    rolled by serger, 45
    rolled hemmer foot, 82
    rolling on jeans, 44
    shirttail, 50
    stretched, 36
    Ultrasuede, 109
    Wonder-Under, 52

Hemstitching
    See Needles
Hill, Marla, 113
Hot pads, 4
Husband
    See Men, sewing for
Increase
    bodice front, 9
Interfacing
    choices, 55
    corduroy, 54
    hems, 52
    where?, 51
    wrinkles, 52
Interfacing, fusible
    cotton, 52
    jacket, 56
    knit, 53
    on collars, 55
    polyesters, 53
    preshrinking, 57
    weft-insertion, 53
Interfacing, sew-in, 52
Interlibrary loan, 12
Invisible elastic, 23
Irons, 58, 84
    Naomoto, 58
    Sussman, 58
Jacket
    button, 17
    interfaced areas, 51
    interfacing, 54, 56
    man's, 1
    Miyake, 20
    ripped seamline, 61
    sewing on buttons, 18
    sleeve ease, 100
    sleeve heads, 95
Jeans
    foot, 66
    hems, 44
Jumpsuit, man's, 62
Knit fusibles
    See Interfacing, fusible
Knits
    buttonholes on, 15
    curling of, 37
Knots, 59
Lace, 60
Ladder stitch, 89
Lapel, 61
    roll line, 17
Leather, 60
Lesage, François, 30
Libraries, 2, 12, 69, 87
Lining
    with fusible interfacing, 56
Lycra®, 38
Machine heirloom sewing,
65
Marking
    darts on lace, 60

McFadden, Mary, 49
Measuring
    sleeve length, 102
Men, sewing for, 1, 61-63
    collar band, 19
    crisp collars, 55
    pants hems, 48
Metropolitan Museum, 108
Miter, double, 20
Mitering, 64
Miyake, Issey, 20
Naomoto iron, 58
Napkins
    rolled hem, 45
Narrowing legs, 69
Neckline
    gap, 9
    piped square, 80
Needle hole, 66
Needles
    for quilting, 85
    wing, 65
New York, 33, 108
Norell, Norman, 21
Off-grain skirt, 35
Osteoporosis, 76
Pants, 37
    bulk on waistbands, 112
    fitting, 67
    hems, 47
    narrowing legs, 69
    stretching, 68
    tummy-control, 38
Patterns
    altering, 1, 9, 73, 76
    Burda, 74
    checking fit, 42
    custom, 62
    designing, 62, 75
    designing , 102
    drafting, 62
    for costumes and theater, 22
    for diagonal designs, 73
    for short people, 69
    from ready-to-wear, 70
    grading, 62, 71
    layouts, 34
    man's shirt, 63
    men's, 62
    sizing, 78
    sleeve ease on, 99
    sloper, 72
Pearls, 90
Pilling
    on cotton/polys, 31
Pin fitting, 42
Piping, 78-79
    square neckline, 80
Placemats, 4, 6-7
Plastic elastic, 23
Pleats
    hems, 44, 49

Polyester
   breathable, 39
   double knit, 37
   fusible interfacing, 53
Preshrinking
   fusible interfacing, 57
Presser feet
   appliqué, 2
   binding, 6-7
   braiding, 78
   buttonhole, 16
   jeans, 66
   rolled hemmer, 82
   rolled hemming, 50
   ruffler, 81
   walking , 85
Presses, 84
   See Irons
Pressing
   collars, 20
   corduroy, 53
   See also Irons
   professional look, 84
   sleeve caps, 101
   wedding gowns, 83
Pricing, 14
Problems
   See your mother
Puckering, 87
Quilting, 85
Ramie, 31
Raveling
   on rolled hems, 45
Remodeling, 86
Repairs
   cigarette burn, 86
Ripples
   in piping, 78
   on curved hems, 50
Rippling
   on buttonholes, 15
Rolled hemming foot, 50
Ruffles, 81, 113, 115
Saint Laurent, Yves, 54-55, 111
Salvaging mistakes, 42, 57, 86
Scarves
   hand-rolled hems, 46
   mitering, 64
Schools, 87
Seam slippage, 42
Seamline
   ripped, 61
   stretched, 36
Seams
   finish, 88
   for toys, 89
   frayed, 88
   puckered, 87
   stress, 43
   Wonder-Under™ for, 52

Sequinned fabric, 93
Sequins and Beads, 90-92
Serger rolled hem, 45
Serging, 88
Sewing
   Ultrasuede, 110
Sewing machine
   blind-hemming, 47
   buttonhole, 17
   buttonholes on, 16-17
   machine-rolled hem, 49
   needle hole, 66
   rolled hemming foot, 50
   stitch length, 105
Shirt
   buttonholes, 16
   curved hems, 50
   interfacing, 55
   man's, 19
   man's pattern, 63
Shirttail curves, 82
Shoulder pads, 94
   dimple , 95
Shrinking
   interfacing, 52
Silk
   fade line, 40
   wild, 42
Skirt
   bias hems, 50
   border print, 31
   bulk on waistband, 112
   crepe de chine, 35
   fraying, 42
   pleats, 44
   puckered, 87
Slacks
   See Pants
Sleeve heads, 23, 95-96
Sleeves
   altering, 97
   ease, 23, 97, 100
   length, 102
   setting, 97
Sloper, 41, 72
Smile lines, 67
Spaghetti straps, 103
Spandex, 38
Spitting iron, 58
Sport coat
   See jacket
Steam
   See Irons
Stitch length, 105
Straps
   spaghetti, 103
Stripes, 42
Suits, men's, 1
Sussman iron, 58
T-shirts, 2-3
   hems, 38
   shortening, 106

Taffeta, 113
Tailor shop, 12
Tailor's knot, 59
Tailoring, 54
   for men, 61
   supplies, 62-63
Tambour embroidery, 30
Test garment, 42
Theatrical costumes
   See Costumes
Thread
   cone, 106
   cotton, 106
   for machine stitching, 107
Thread tracing, 70
Topstitching
   elastic, 27
Toy seam, 89
Train, 113
Travel
   New York City, 108
Trousers
   See Pants
Ultrasuede, 2-3, 52
   coat, 109
   hem, 109
Underlining
   with fusible interfacing, 56
Waistbands
   bulk, 112
   casings, 28
   distributing fullness, 25
   drawstring elastic for, 24
   elasticized, 26
   invisible elastic for, 23
   tight, 111
Walking foot, 85
Wedding dress
   applying beads, 90
   gathering ruffles, 113
   train on, 113
Weddings, 113
Width
   bodice front, 9
Wonder-Under
   hems, 52
Wool
   boiled, 39
Wrinkles
   bust, 8-9
   in pants, 67
   in sleeves, 9
   interfacing, 52
   on cotton, 52
   on piping, 80
Zippers
   heavy-duty, 116
   self-basting, 116

Preface

I've collected sewing "problems" for years. In fact, that's one reason I became a writer—I couldn't find the answers to my own questions. Through the years, my collection of questions has grown tremendously, thanks to my students at the College of the Desert, home sewers I've met in all parts of the United States, and *Sew News* readers who responded to my S.O.S. column.

This book is a collection of some of my favorites. If it doesn't answer *your* question, let me know, so that I can answer in my new column in *Sewing Update Newsletter* and include it in a future S.O.S. volume (see last page for address).

I welcome your questions, because I love sewing! For me, the challenge of sewing, solving problems, developing new techniques, learning industry methods, and researching are just as exciting as wearing a new design I've made.

This book was written because I can't visit each of you personally. I hope you will *use* it—underline and write notes in it; update it with tips you pick up in your reading and sewing; cross-reference subjects with the page numbers of similar information in your favorite books. Imagine me sitting next to you with my words of advice and encouragement. Let me share with you the joy of sewing.

Claire Shaeffer
Palm Springs, CA

Foreword

From the very beginning, we envisioned *Sew News* as a lively journal, where people who love to sew could exchange ideas and be inspired to try something new. We created a laboratory setting, where all sorts of ideas—new and old—were discussed. A mix of tested technique and artistic expression, *Sew News* articles gave readers a cornucopia of ideas from which to choose.

Yet our adventurous, creative home-sewing readers clamored for even more information about how to solve problems and duplicate design techniques. It took us over a year to find someone as qualified as Claire Shaeffer.

Her design talent and common sense were rooted in teaching. Hours in the laboratory with students gave her proven solutions to all sorts of sewing problems. She knew first-hand what real problems sewers ran into and how frustrating a simple-to-solve problem could be.

Of the hundreds of articles we printed, none drew so much reader response as Claire Shaeffer's question-and-answer columns. Claire's ability to explain clearly, concisely, and with a passion that inspired readers made her "Sewing S.O.S" column one of the most well-read pages of *Sew News*. Claire's lively intellect, curiosity, and creative talent exemplified the best of *Sew News* and its readers.

This new book, a compilation of her work, gives readers the right answers to sewing problems and the inspiration to keep learning, experimenting, and creating beautiful things.

Laura Rehrmann
Founding Editor, "Sew News"

How To Use This Book

Plenty of sewing books tell us what we *should* do; not many acknowledge that things can go wrong—but they do, even to experienced home sewers. And when things go wrong, it's often difficult to unearth the information we need. Either the books have a poor index or worse, none, or they skip over the gremlins.

The purpose of this book is to streamline the process of sewing for you. We've deliberately designed the book with generous margins, so that you really *use* the book for a long time.

Instead of clipping columns and tips by Claire and other sewing writers and then tossing them into a bulging, disorganized file, use this book as your organizing skeleton. Paste or staple the clippings in the proper alphabetical listing. Then cross-index them in the Index at the front of the book.

We've also included a Resource List at the end. When you order a product from a company or see an ad for something interesting, enter the information: no more searching all your books and magazines for one address.

Likewise, if there's a page or two in several different books that you return to again and again—how to make shoulder pads, how to miter a corner, etc.—we encourage you to photocopy or copy the information and file it alphabetically in here. Add your own favorite books to the Bibliography.

When you run into trouble and want to find help in this book, look first to the Index. We've tried to figure out every key word you might use, so that we can direct you to where we've placed Claire's answer.

In general, we've used nouns and garment parts as our organizing principles. For example, if you have a question about wrinkles on pants, we classified it under Pants and cross-indexed it under Wrinkles and Slacks. Look at the bold entries in the Table of Contents for our major categories.

Most of all, we hope this book is a helpful addition to your sewing library.

Robbie Fanning
Publisher

*Note: We thank Sew News, where Claire's column originally appeared, and **Sewing Update Newsletter**, where her column now appears, for permission to reprint these questions and answers. Their addresses are at the end of the Resource List.*

Alterations

Q How do you alter men's suits to fit a lady? Are there any books on this subject?

A To my knowledge, there is no book. If you want to use the lapel, buttonholes and pockets of the man's jacket, plan your new garment around them. Then, rip the old garment apart so that you can lay it out flat. Place your pattern on the flat garment or garment sections, aligning the seamlines on the pattern with the finished edges of the jacket you want to change. If possible, match the grainlines on the pattern and garment. Cut, mark, and reassemble the jacket.

This isn't difficult to master; however, it will require patience, some creativity, and a bit of experimentation.

Use this technique if dieting has reduced your girth several sizes. If you're altering a garment which you tailored, use the same pattern in a smaller size (either learn to grade it yourself—see Patterns— or buy it). Discontinued patterns can sometimes be purchased directly from the pattern company. See the Resource List at the end of the book for addresses.

See the next question for books on altering clothes in general.

See also Men, Patterns.

Q I'm in the alterations business and need books on clothing alteration. Can you help?

A There is no comprehensive book on how to alter, but these publications might help (see Bibliography for full annotation):

• *Altering Ready-To-Wear Fashions*, Jeanne Brinkley and Ann Aletti.

A

Alterations

- *Altering Men's Ready-to-Wear*, Mary A. Roehr.
- *Altering Women's Ready-to-Wear*, Mary A. Roehr.
- *Mary Johnson's Guide to Altering and Restyling Ready-Made Clothes*, Mary Johnson.
- *Discover Dressmaking as a Professional Career*, James C. Leiter, Jr., and Joan Stanley.
- *Price It Right*, Claire Shaeffer.
- "Sewing for Profit," Bulletin #208, Cooperative Extension Service, Ohio State University.
- *Sewing as a Home Business*, Mary A. Roehr.
- "Yes, You Can Alter Ready-to-Wear," Belle Rivers.

In addition, your county agent may have pertinent brochures. Cooperative Extension Services are listed in the county offices section of your local telephone book or ask a reference librarian.

See also Bodice, Business, Fit, Men, Pants, Patterns, Waistbands, Zippers.

Appliqué

Q When I make a satin stitch around Ultrasuede® appliqués on T-shirts, the stitches are uneven and the bobbin thread shows. Can you help?

A These suggestions should help you get the best appliqués using Ultrasuede®:

- Use an appliqué foot, preferably with a Teflon bottom. If you can't find one, spray the bottom of the appliqué foot with Elmer's Slide-All® or another dry spray lubricant.
- Tighten the bobbin tension and/or loosen upper tension. You will have to experiment to see what works. The top thread

A

should be pulled to the underside, not vice versa. If you have a removable bobbin case and appliqué frequently, consider buying an extra bobbin case. One can be used for standard garment sewing and the second for appliqué and machine embroidery, where you will fiddle with bobbin tension often (mark this case with red nail polish).

- Make several samples, loosening or tightening top and bobbin tension as needed, until you like what you see.
- You could also satin stitch the Ultrasuede® separately and then attach it to the T-shirt at the inner edge of the satin stitch with a straight stitch.

See also Ultrasuede.

Appliqué

B

Batting

Q I want to purchase asbestos backing to make placemats and hot pads. I've seen many patterns for making these items, but I haven't been able to locate any backing that will absorb heat.

A Asbestos backing is not available. I use a polyester batting with insulating qualities called Needlepunch Insulation. It's lightweight, doesn't require quilting, can be machine-washed and -dried, and will protect your hands from hot pots and your table from hot dishes. (See the Resource List for sources.)

Some people cut up Teflon ironing board covers and use them inside placemats and hot pads.

See also Bindings.

B

Q Can I make a belt with a buckle without inserting stiff 1"-wide belting into a tube?

A For a professional-looking belt, have the belt made by a professional beltmaker. The cost will be slightly more than making it yourself, but the results are well worth it. Many fabric retailers and shoe-repair shops offer this service, or write Fashion Touches (see Resource List) for a free catalog.

If you're in a hurry, try this. Cut one fabric belt 1" wider and 1" longer than the finished measurements. Cut two pieces of Stacy's Craft-Fuse® the width and length of the finished belt. With the fabric wrong side up, center and fuse one Craft-Fuse® piece to the fabric belt (see first illustration). Miter the corners of the fabric at the belt point and press all seam allowances to the wrong side (see second illustration). Trim the second piece of Craft-Fuse® 1/8" on all sides; fuse it to the back of the belt. Topstitch around the belt, make the eyelets, and add the buckle.

Q The belt on one of my favorite dresses always slips out of the buckle. The underside of the belt is vinyl and it's difficult to sew on snaps or Velcro®. What do you recommend?

A Try gluing Velcro® to the belt with Velcro® Adhesive. It works beautifully.

Belts and Buckles

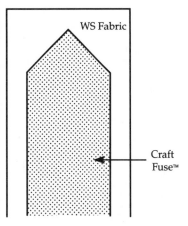

WS Fabric

Craft Fuse™

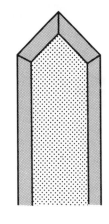

Bias

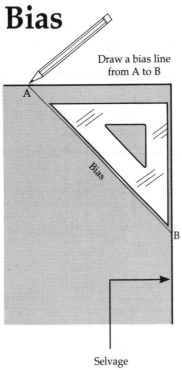

Draw a bias line
from A to B

A

Bias

B

Selvage

Bindings

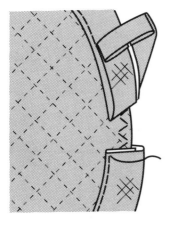

Q How do you find the bias on permanent-press broadcloth? It's difficult because the crossgrain is not perpendicular to the selvage.

A The grains are permanently set in position on permanent-press materials, and the crossgrain may or may not be at right angles to the selvage or lengthwise grain. Even if you can pull and tug the material so the crossgrain is perpendicular to the selvage, the threads will not remember this new position and will return to the positions they had when they received the permanent-press finish.

To establish the bias, use a 90° triangle. Position one short side on the selvage or straight grain. Use chalk or a temporary marking pen to draw a line at the triangle base.

Q What is the easiest way to bind the edges of placemats?

A There are several ways to apply bias bindings. For placemats, I particularly like the three methods described below. First, though, cut out the placemats and for easy handling, zigzag (stitch width 2, stitch length 2) around each edge.

- Purchase or make double-fold binding the desired width. Use a steam iron to shape the bias so it will fit the curves smoothly. Beginning at one side, slip the placemat between the folds of the binding, so the larger fold is on the bottom. Baste the binding around the placemat with a water-soluble glue stick. Allow the ends to overlap 1" and fold the end under 1/4". Using the inside of the presser foot as a guide, topstitch the binding in place (see first illustration).

B

Bindings

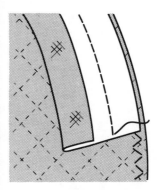

- Double-fold or regular bias binding may be used for this application. Open out the binding. With the placemat wrong side up and the binding on top, stitch a 1/4" seam (see second illustration). Wrap the binding around the edge of the mat, glue-baste and press. Topstitch the binding in place (see third illustration).

- If you apply bindings frequently, try using one of the newer binding presser feet (see fourth illustration). Unlike older versions, the newer feet really work and require only minimal practice to achieve professional results. One I like from Tread-leart (see Resource List) can be adjusted for double-fold bindings up to 1" wide. Be sure it fits your machine, though, since it's only made for a short-shank machine.

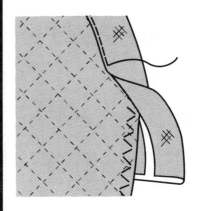

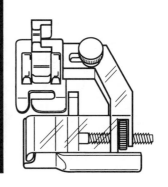

Sewing S.O.S. 7

B

Bodice

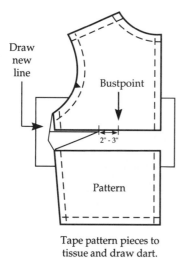

Draw new line

Bustpoint

2" - 3"

Pattern

Tape pattern pieces to tissue and draw dart.

Q I have a large bust. How can I add darts to dartless designs?

A I've found the add-and-fit method to be most successful.

- Try on a blouse that doesn't have bust darts. Stand in front of a full-length mirror. Note diagonal wrinkles extending downward from the bust point to the underarm seam (see first illustration).

- Pin a bust dart, making it about 2" wide at the underarm seam. Disregard the blouse back, examining only the way the garment hangs in front.

- Have the original wrinkles disappeared or been reduced? If not, repin the darts until the blouse hangs straight below the bust (see second illustration). For larger busts, the end of the dart should be 2" to 3" from the bust point. If the dart extends beyond the largest part of the bust, the dart will look crooked.

- Once you've determined dart placement, remove the blouse and measure the total amount pinned out at the underarm seam.

- Make a dart insert: on pattern paper, draw two parallel lines the same distance apart as the pinned-out measurement.

- Now use your dart insert on your pattern. Locate the bustpoint. If one is not indicated on the pattern, hold it up to your body, find the bustpoint, and mark it with a felt-tipped pen.

- Draw a line at a right angle to the center front and through the bustpoint.

- Cut the pattern apart and tape the dart insert to the pattern sections.

- Draw the new bust dart (see third illustration).

- Fold the the dart into its finished position. True the side seam by trimming the side seam tissue at the cutting line.

To alter a blouse you've already cut out, fit the blouse and mark the dart before the stitching the side seams. The darts will shorten the front. Trim the back as needed to match the front.

Q How do you alter the front bodice to eliminate horizontal wrinkles over the bust?

A Wrinkles are inherent to some sleeve designs, such as kimono, raglan, or dolman. Therefore, I assume you are asking about set-in sleeves.

Generally, horizontal wrinkles form when a garment rides up because it is too tight. This is frequently a problem if you have a large bust cup size.

To solve this problem, increase the width of the bodice *front* in the bust area; and, if needed, add a bust dart (see illustrations). If your pattern doesn't show a bust point, hold the tissue up to your body and mark the bust point. Then follow the directions in the first question in the Bodice section for adding a dart.

See also Fit, Patterns.

Q My garments gap at the neckline. Do you have a solution?

A Neckline "gaposis" can be caused by a variety of figure irregularities, including a small neck, square shoulders, small bust, or a dowager's hump; however, gaposis can be corrected.

Bodice

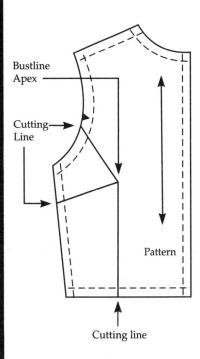

Bustline Apex — Cutting Line — Pattern — Cutting line

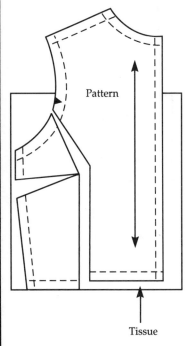

Pattern — Tissue

Bodice

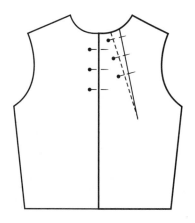

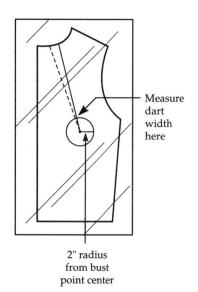

Measure dart width here

2" radius from bust point center

Select a pattern with a front opening and jewel (high round) neckline. Make a fitting muslin from this pattern, cutting out the front and back sections from muslin, stay stitching the necklines carefully, and joining at the shoulder and underarm seams.

To ensure accuracy, have a friend help you fit the muslin.

Try on the garment and pin it together at the center front. Clip the neckline seam allowance only as needed so the muslin will fit smoothly.

Remove the excess fabric in the gaping neckline by pinning a dart from the neckline to the bust point (see first illustration).

Take the garment off. Use a pencil to mark the side of the dart at each pin. Remove the pins and rip the muslin apart, so the darted section will lie flat.

To transfer the fitting dart to your pattern front, lay the muslin on the table and cover it with the tissue pattern. Carefully trace the marked dart lines onto the tissue. Using the bust point as the center, draw a circle with a 2" radius. Measure the width of the fitting dart on the circle and record this information for future reference (use the margins on this page, if you wish). (See second illustration.)

Note: If the dart doesn't extend to the bust point, measure the distance between the end of the dart and the bust point and record for later use.

Slash the pattern on one of the marked dart lines almost, but not quite, to the bust point.

If the pattern has a bust dart, slash through its center almost to the bust point. If the pattern doesn't have a bust dart, slash the pattern from the hem almost to the bust point. To close the fitting dart, match the dart legs

B

and tape them together. (See third illustration.)

When you compare the adjusted pattern to the original, the length of the neckline will be shorter. Also, the shoulder seam will have less slant and the original bust dart will be larger.

If your pattern doesn't have a bust dart, closing the fitting dart will increase the pattern width below the bust. If this is unwanted, remove the excess at the side seam by trimming away an amount equal to the increase. (See fourth illustration.)

You should now have a well-fitted pattern. Necklines vary, of course, and the width of the fitting dart at the neckline will decrease when the neckline is lowered; therefore, you must determine the dart size. Either measure the angle of the dart at the tip with a protractor or measure the dart width at a given point. For example, you have already measured and recorded the width of the dart 2" from the bust point.

To use this alteration on other patterns, copy the bust circle and dart width. Slash from the neckline through the fitting dart and proceed as above.

Q What is a good sewing dictionary and where can I buy one?

A *The Thread-Line* is an excellent, easy-to-use dictionary with over 1,000 terms relating to sewing and needlecrafts. It was written by Susan Gaino-Roberts for adult education students and published by Jefferson County Adult Education (see Bibliography for all book annotations).

The Dressmaker's Dictionary by English author Ann Ladbury is a reference book arranged in

Bodice

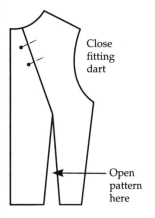

Close fitting dart

Open pattern here

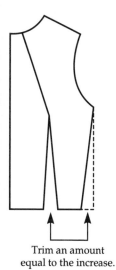

Trim an amount equal to the increase.

Books

B

Books

alphabetical order. However, this book is difficult to use as it doesn't include an index. Also, it is sometimes confusing because many of the terms are British.

I have included a Fiber and Fabric Dictionary in my new book, *Claire Shaeffer's Fabric Sewing Guide.* See last page.

Q I ordered a book mentioned in one of your columns and I don't like it. Do you read the books you mention? Can I return it?

A Yes, I do read every book I mention, in addition to many I never mention. Sometimes I don't like a book, but I will mention it anyway. When a good book is not available on a subject in question, I feel obligated to relay what is available to my readers, despite my opinion.

Most companies, even book clubs, will allow you to return a book if it is still in new condition, although they probably will not refund the postage. Write the customer service department, explain why you are unhappy, and ask how to return the book.

In the future, when you wonder if a book is worth buying, visit your local library. Most libraries belong to an interlibrary loan system that allows them to borrow books from larger libraries anywhere in the United States.

See also the Bibliography at the end of the book.

Business

Q I want to turn my sewing hobby into a career. I'd prefer to start as an apprentice in a tailor shop. Can you suggest an organization to contact or a publication to advertise in about getting an apprenticeship?

A Word of mouth and pounding the pavement are the best ways to get an appren-

B

Business

ticeship in a tailoring shop. Visit tailoring shops and talk to tailors, but be sure to call first. Don't be discouraged if they are doubtful about hiring a home sewer—this is usual. Take any job you're offered in a tailoring shop, as you'll learn a lot merely by watching.

You also might consider a job in the alterations department of a men's store or a large department store. This will give you an opportunity to learn from ready-to-wear construction.

Q I have many years of sewing and book-keeping experience and would like to start a fabric store that offers classes in sewing. I need direction on how to get started, where to purchase inventory, etc.

A Start by visiting as many fabric stores as possible to learn what sort of image you want for your store. Then talk to the owner of the store most suited to your style. Be prepared to pay for his or her time—it will be well worth the money. Ask the owner if she would consider helping you start a non-competing store, and if so, how much a consultation would cost and what it would include. If you want consultations with more than one owner, be sure you aren't asking for trade secrets from a potential competitor.

See also the next question.

Q A friend is starting a shop to supply flags, costumes, and other accessories to bands and drum-and-bugle corps. Can you recommend a resource or directory for fabrics and supplies?

A You must know where to purchase supplies *before* you go into business.

B

Business

The American Home Sewing Association sponsors annual trade shows for the home-sewing market. The shows are held on both coasts in the Spring and Fall (only for those who possess a resale number and business license, not for consumers). Fabric manufacturers and suppliers exhibit their products and take orders. Many require minimum opening orders. For more information, write AHSA (see Resource List).

"Sew Business," a trade magazine for storeowners, publishes an annual directory of resources, as does "The Homesewing Trade News."

Q I'm a good custom dressmaker. My customers are very pleased with their finished garments, but many think my prices are too high. It takes time to make and fit a quality garment and I have some overhead expenses, even though I work out of my home. How do I justify my pricing to my customers?

A Before you start justifying, consider your customers. Custom garments are not for bargain hunters. When your customer indicates she can buy ready-to-wear for less, encourage her to do so. But if she wants a one-of-a-kind design in a particular color that fits her perfectly, start talking.

Typical custom-design customers have unusual or difficult-to-fit figures, can't find appropriate garments for work, or want distinctive designs. Generally, they're willing to pay higher prices when they have purchased expensive fabrics. Even so, they sometimes forget the current minimum wage for unskilled labor—and custom dressmaking is anything but unskilled labor. Be sure to compare the quality of your work to equal quality ready-to-wear.

B

Business

Give your customer choices about the garment's construction. You can pare the price by eliminating linings, underlinings, shoulder pads, lingerie straps, time-consuming hem and seam finishes, etc. Price optionals as extras so she can choose those most important to her. Encourage her to order two or more garments with the same design and offer a discount (but charge extra for difficult-to-handle fabrics).

If your customer has a fitting problem, show her, using your alteration pricing guide, how much it costs to alter ready-to-wear garments and point out the advantages of custom garments.

Custom sewing is an art, whether it is alterations or complete garment construction. In my opinion, self-employed dressmakers should make $8-10 per hour (before expenses). Some make considerably more. Many, regrettably, make less.

Naturally, in order to charge higher prices, your business must be run professionally: neatly dressed employees; an adequate and private fitting area; neat clutter in your workroom; specified business hours (not only when it suits you); deliveries ready when promised; a minimum of socializing; no children running in and out; no television; and, of course, professional work.

See also Alterations, Men.

Buttonholes

Q What can I do to prevent rippling buttonholes on knit fabrics?

A Buttonholes often ripple when placed parallel to the crossgrain on woven fabrics or on the course (rib) of knits. Prevent this by cording the buttonholes.

B

Buttonholes

Use a heavy, cord-like topstitching thread, buttonhole twist, pearl cotton, or four strands of regular thread for cording. If you're using regular thread, wax it; then twist the four strands together to make the cording.

Some buttonhole presser feet have a device on the back or front to hook the extra thread on. This allows you to zigzag easily over the cord without stitching through it. With a little practice, you can learn to guide the cording by hand if you don't have such a foot.

Pull the threads slightly after the buttonhole is completed. Then use a calyx-eyed or large-eyed needle to pull the threads to the underside. Knot and bury the thread ends in the underside of the buttonhole. Clip any extra thread.

Other important ways to reduce rippling are to interface the buttonhole area and to stitch with a stabilizer between the fabric and feed dogs. I sometimes use a single layer of a Ziploc® bag as a stabilizer. I also like water-soluble stabilizer.

Q On my new sewing machine, I can set the stitch length for one buttonhole and it will make all the others the same size. Recently, I made a shirt and all of the buttonholes were the same size except the one on the collar band. What happened?

A Your machine counts the number of stitches in the first buttonhole to determine the size of all the buttonholes. If the bulk of the fabric impedes the progress of the presser foot, stitches will pile up in one place. Meanwhile, the machine is counting the number of stitches it has made. It may make the right number of stitches—but the buttonhole will be 1/8" short. This can also happen if you are stitching half the buttonhole on hidden

B

seam allowances and half on only two layers of fabric.

The seam allowances in the collar band probably caused your problem. Next time don't use the machine's memory for the buttonhole on the collar band. Stitch it manually.

Buttonholes

Q My new computer sewing machine allows me to narrow the bead of the buttonhole, which I like very much—but it leaves more exposed fabric in the center of the buttonhole. When I cut the buttonhole open, wisps of threads stick out after the first washing. How should I trim the inside of the buttonhole?

A From Wonder-Under™, Fine Fuse™, or TransFuse™II, cut a rectangle 1/4" by the length of the buttonhole plus an extra 1/4". With the front section wrong side side up, center the fusible over the buttonhole location; fuse it in place before attaching the facing. Attach the facings and fuse the layers together. Machine stitch and carefully cut the buttonholes parallel to the crossgrain.

See also Interfacing.

Buttons

Q The top button on many jackets is too low for me. When I move it up, the lapel doesn't roll properly. Can you help?

A The top button and lapel roll line are designed together. Unfortunately, you can't change one without changing the other—and it's preferable not to change either. You might find it simpler to choose a different jacket style, unless you are prepared to make both alterations.

B

Buttons

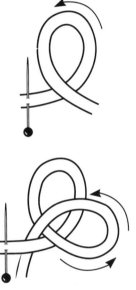

Q How can I sew on metal buttons so they'll be less likely to fall off? I have some lovely monogrammed buttons but they need to be resewn frequently and I'm always afraid I'll lose one.

A Metal buttons and buttons with metal shanks actually cut through the threads that secure them, when the buttons are buttoned and unbuttoned.

A good method for securing buttons with shanks is to thread the eye of a hook and eye into the button shank; then sew the eye in place at the button location. The combined shank and eye should be as thick as the jacket front; use straight eyes on lightweight garments and curved eyes on heavier, thicker garments.

Q I like the look of Chinese ball buttons? Are they easy to make?

A Yes, Chinese ball buttons are easy to make and add an attractive accent to your garments. They are generally made from self-fabric bias tubing or from purchased cording. The size of the finished button varies according to the size of the tubing. I find buttons with diameters between 1/4" and 1" most attractive; therefore, I prefer to use bias tubings made from lightweight silky fabrics.

For each button, you'll need approximately 10" of tubing. Make the first loop. Make the second loop over and under the first loop. Make the third loop, weaving through the first two. Pull gently to shape the button into a ball. Trim away the excess tubing and sew the ends to the underside of the button. (See illustration.)

Collars

Q I have a problem sewing shirts for my husband. When sewing the collar band to the front of the shirt, the collar band is always slightly larger at the end and "bumps out." How can I correct this?

A By using the same technique you probably use at the ends of waistbands, you can avoid bumps at the end of collar bands.

- Stitch the collar band to the neckline *before* stitching the ends of the band.
- Using a short stitch, complete the ends of the bands; grade the seam allowances; and trim the ends to 1/8".

Two-piece shirt collars are easier to apply if you shuffle the construction sequence. Is this the sequence you're now using?

- Complete the collar.
- Join the collar to one band section.
- Join the collar/band to the other band section and complete the ends of the band.
- Stitch one band to the garment neckline.
- Turn in the seam allowance at the bottom of the other band and topstitch it in place.

The following sequence works better. The seam allowance turned in at the end is a concave curve, which is easier to finish smoothly than the convex curve at the lower edge of the band.

- Complete the collar.
- Join the collar to one band section.
- Join the collar/band to the garment neckline.
- Join the remaining band section to the garment neckline.
- Complete the ends of the collar.
- Turn in the seam allowances at the top of the band and stitch in place.

See also Buttonholes, Men.

Collars

Q I recently made an Issey Miyake unlined jacket. I followed the pattern exactly, but the collar corners are very bulky and look homemade. What can I do?

A The construction technique for this collar hem is an authentic Miyake design—the hem is folded over twice and topstitched in place. This leaves five layers of fabric at the corners. If your fabric is thick or bulky, this hem might be unattractive.

Sometimes, the garment appearance can be improved with a good pressing. Place your garment on a sturdy pressing table or cover the floor with a sheet. Using a steam iron and a damp press cloth, fill each corner with steam; then pound vigorously with a clapper. Do not move the collar until it has dried thoroughly. Woolens and a few other fabrics will look better if you protect the garment with two self-fabric press cloths placed just above and below the garment. Always experiment on scraps first.

If pressing doesn't solve the problem, you can change the method of construction and reduce bulk by using a double miter. You will need a 1-1/8" hem allowance to make a finished hem 1/2" wide—some width will be lost with the turn of the cloth.

Fold the hems on the paper pattern exactly as they will be sewn; then, using a ruler and tracing wheel, mark the miter seamline from the corner to the point where the two hems meet. Open the pattern and indicate 1/4" seam allowances for the corner seam (see illustration). Trim away the excess paper.

When assembling the garment, fold the corner right sides together, stitch on the seamline, press the seam open, and turn the corner right side out. Press hem in place and topstitch.

See also Mitering.

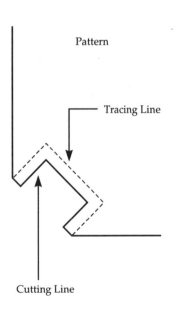

Pattern

Tracing Line

Cutting Line

Q My bias tie collar looks wonderful, except where I stitched the seams at the ends. Both ends are about 1/2" wider than the rest of the tie. What did I do?

A You probably inadvertently stretched the ends while stitching. Designer Norman Norell frequently uses the following detail, which you may also find helpful.

Make the ends of both ties 2" longer than the pattern. Finish the collar except for the ends. Mark and measure a distance 2-5/8" from each end, then carefully fold the ends into the tie and press (see illustrations). The ends are not stitched closed, thus avoiding any stretching.

See also Interfacing.

Collars

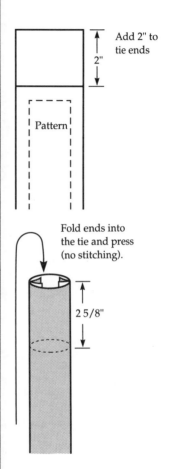

Add 2" to tie ends

2"

Pattern

Fold ends into the tie and press (no stitching).

2 5/8"

Q I have been asked to make costumes for the high-school drama deparment. Although I am a very good seamstress, I'm more than a little apprehensive. What do you recommend?

A There are several good books on costume design and each has its own strengths. All of the following books should be available through interlibrary loan if your local library doesn't have them. (See Bibliography for annotations.)

• *Costume Design*, Barbara and Cletus Anderson, is a textbook that explains the prin-

Costumes

C

Costumes

ciples of developing patterns, selecting fabrics and colors, and costume characterization. It is somewhat overwhelming for amateur costumers, but is an excellent resource for budding professionals.

- *The Costumer's Handbook*, Rosemary Ingham and Elizabeth Covey, is especially good. It focuses on techniques for designing, fitting, and sewing theatrical costumes, with a particularly helpful shopping guide.

- *The Costume Designer's Handbook*, Rosemary Ingham and Elizabeth Covey, is a guide for both amateur and professional costume designers. It includes an extensive shopping guide and excellent information on researching period costumes.

- *Patterns for Theatrical Costumes*, Katherine Strand Holkeboer, includes costume patterns from ancient Egypt to 1915.

- *Sewing and Collecting Vintage Fashions*, Eileen MacIntosh, is a new book from Chilton, written especially for home sewers. It has an extensive resource list and bibliography.

- "Bias Line" is a good newsletter for costumers. It is published eleven times a year and contains pattern and construction ideas, complete details for developing patterns, and a question-and-answer column that deals with a variety of problems.

Creases

Q I want to remove a permanent-press crease from a cotton-blend fabric. I've applied white vinegar directly to the fabric and pressed it with a dry iron without success. Any suggestions?

A The "crease" may actually be a fade line. If that's the case, nothing will remove it. Before you admit defeat, wet the fabric again with undiluted white vinegar, cover it with brown paper strips and press until dry.

Ease

Q How much ease should I allow in the cap of a set-in sleeve?

A With most fabrics, I prefer a minimum of 1" ease in sleeve caps. When the ease is less than 1", the sleeve will not hang properly. (If the sleeve is short, you can allow as little as 1/2" without distorting the hang of the sleeve.) Some fabrics are more difficult to ease than others. For difficult-to-ease fabrics like permanent-press cotton or cotton/polyester, I sometimes cut the sleeves on the bias.

Use this quick-and-easy sleeve head to improve the cap's appearance on difficult-to-ease fabrics.

- Cut a 1-1/2" x 8" bias strip from muslin or interfacing.
- Pin the strip into the top of the sleeve, centering it over the seam line.
- With the garment on top, secure the strip by hand or machine on the original seam line.

See also Sleeve Heads, Sleeves.

Elastic

Q My sewing friends are excited about something called invisible elastic. What is it and how do I apply it?

A Sometimes referred to as "plastic elastic," invisible elastic is made of a clear material that looks like a strip of opaque cellophane. It appears to be a home sewer's dream come true. It is lightweight, supple, chlorine-safe, and available in 1/4" and 3/8" widths. When applied directly to the fabric with a zigzag stitch, it doesn't grow, but recovers to its original length. With a stretch ratio of more than 100%, it's suitable for either conventional or serger sewing. If your local retailer doesn't stock it, it can be ordered from Clotilde and other mail-order companies (see Resource List).

E

Elastic

Q How is 1-1/4"-wide drawstring elastic best applied?

A Designed to eliminate the time-consuming process of inserting drawstrings in ready-to-wear and to make garments with adjustable waistbands, drawstring elastic is ideal for the waistbands of activewear, athleticwear, and pajama pants. It can also be used anywhere the extra power of a pulled-and-fastened drawcord is wanted.

Although drawstring elastic can be applied in several ways, it's best to apply it like lingerie elastic. Understand that both the cord and the elastic will stretch; in fact, the elastic has 100% stretch.

- To apply, cut the elastic the same size as the waist measurement.
- Pull out the drawstring 1/2" from each end. Knot each end. Join only the elastic ends, not the cord. Finger press the seam open; topstitch each side.
- Divide the elastic into eighths and mark with pins.
- Stitch the garment together following pattern instructions.
- Fold under the top raw edge of the garment 5/8" and press.
- Make two vertical buttonhole openings at the front of the garment. Space them 1" apart and 5/8" from the folded edge. The drawcord will be drawn through these holes at the front of the garment.
- Divide the top edge of the garment into eighths and mark with pins.
- Pin the upper edge of the elastic to the inside of the garment, matching edges evenly and matching all pin markers. Be certain the elastic seam is at the center front of the garment. Using a straight stitch, sew the elastic to the garment along the upper edge of the elastic and the garment,

stretching each section of elastic to fit the garment and stitching one section at a time. Repeat along the bottom edge of the elastic.

- For a smooth finish, stitch two more rows through the fabric and elastic—one slightly below the cord and one slightly above the cord. *Note:* Do not sew into or through the drawcord portion of the elastic, as this will prevent the drawcord from pulling through.

- Reach through the buttonhole opening with a tapestry needle or crochet hook and pull the knotted ends of the drawcord out of the elastic and through to the outside of the garment.

Q I'm having trouble distributing the fulness of the elastic evenly in the waistbands of dresses. I've tried sewing the bodice and skirt seam allowances together to make a casing, and I've tried making a separate casing using wide bias tape. All the fullness still remains on the first half of the elastic. Can you help?

A Use a slippery material to make the casing, make the casing 1/4" wider than the elastic, and use a braided elastic that narrows when stretched. All of these methods will help you to easily slide the elastic through the casing.

Sewing the seam allowances together to make a casing isn't always the best method. It's often bulky, unattractive at the waist, and too narrow for the elastic. When you don't want to make a separate casing, use a topstitched seam to create a casing.

For separate or applied casings, cut the casing from Seams Great® or Seams-Saver™, from scraps of silk or silky fabrics, or from scraps of nylon tricot.

Elastic

Q I do custom sewing for many older ladies who like elasticized waistbands. Can you use elastic to interface waistbands? If so, how?

A Elasticized waistbands are comfortable, and they're perfect for those with fluctuating waistlines. This method, utilizing 1"-wide elastic, is effective.

- To determine the waistband length, start with the largest waist measurement and add two seam allowances (1-1/4"). Cut the band this length on the lengthwise grain, using the selvage as one long edge if possible.

- Using the smallest waist measurement, measure and cut the elastic.

- If the band doesn't have a selvage, finish one long edge by serging or zigzagging it (width, 3; length, 2). With right sides together, join the unfinished edge of the band to the skirt or pants. With the garment right side up, place the elastic on top of the seam allowances, matching the lower edge of the elastic to the seamline (see first illustration). Pin the elastic to the seam allowances at each end of the band.

- Distribute the fullness as desired. Then pin and stitch the elastic to the side seam, so the fabric won't slip (see second illustration). Most garments will be more attractive if the band is smooth in the front with the fullness concentrated in the back only.

- With right sides together, stitch the ends of the band, catching the elastic in the seamline(see third illustration).

- Turn the band right side out. Baste the band in place. With the garment right side up, stitch in the ditch to finish it.

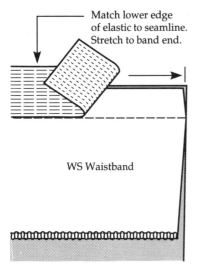

Match lower edge of elastic to seamline. Stretch to band end.

WS Waistband

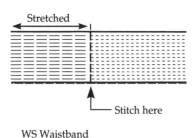

Stretched

Stitch here

WS Waistband

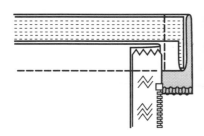

Elastic

Q When I topstitch several times through elastic in waistbands on shorts or skirts, the waist is always too large. This doesn't seem to be a problem in ready-to-wear garments. What am I doing wrong?

A This is a good-news, bad-news answer. The good news is the problem can be solved; the bad news is the solution will take time, effort, and patience.

One of the biggest problems faced by manufacturers in the fashion industry is that when you machine stitch through elastic, it loses some of its recovery and will never return to its original length. Depending on the type and manufacturer, the elastic will "grow" 1/16" to 1/4" for every 2" used.

To determine how much the elastic will grow, cut a 4" piece and mark a 2" section in the center area. Stitch the elastic to the fabric without stretching it, until you reach the first mark. Then stretch the elastic as much as possible and stitch to the second. Stitch to the end of the elastic without any more stretching. Remeasure the marked center area. Let's assume it now measures 2-1/4" (see illustration).

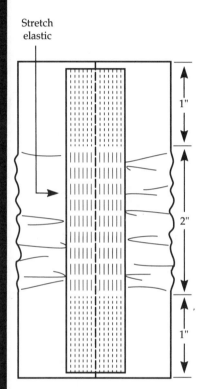

Stretch elastic

Now you must determine how much shorter to cut the elastic so that it will grow to match your waist measurement. To determine the needed length, divide the growth measurement (2-1/4") by the original measurement (2"). This equals 1.125. Let's say your waist measurement is 30". Divide it by 1.125, which equals 26-3/4" (round off fractions to the nearest 1/4").

Now you're ready to make a test garment. Lap the ends 1/2" and join them. Stitch the elastic into the garment and check the fit. If it is too tight or too loose, rip it out or make another test garment. Repeat until the length is right. Congratulations! You have just become a samplemaker.

Elastic

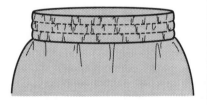

Mark foldlines and
seam allowances.

WS
Waistband

Seam
allowance

Foldline

Seam
allowance

WS
Waistband

Leave
opening
for elastic
insertion.

So that you don't have to repeat this every time you use the same elastic, record all of this information (including the kind of elastic used) on the pattern envelope or in the margin of this book.

Q I always have trouble sliding elastic into waistline casings. Is there an easier way?

A A reader of my old "Sew News" column shared this technique. Cut the desired length of elastic into two equal sections. Thread one into the casing of the front and one into the back of a dress before stitching the side seams.

Of course you must plan ahead. Before fitting the garment, place and stitch the casing into position. Also, decide whether the bulk of the elastic ends at the side seams will be uncomfortable to you.

Q How can I duplicate the popular ready-to-wear waistband look featuring multiple rows of elastic?

A Frequently used by designers, this waistband features several rows of 1/8"- to 1/4"-wide elastic in individual casings (see first illustration).

- Cut the band fabric 3-3/4" wide and long enough to pull over your hips easily. Add seam allowances to the length (see second illustration).
- Make short clips on the band ends to mark the center foldline and seamlines.
- With right sides together, stitch the short ends of the waistband from one edge to 1/16" beyond the foldline clip. Backstitch. Then stitch from the seamline snip to the edge (see third illustration). Press the seam open. The unstitched section will

form the opening needed to insert the elastic.

- Gather the skirt, if necessary, using two rows of gathering stitches along the skirt seamline. Divide and mark the band and skirt into eighths, so the fullness will be evenly distributed. Pull gathers to fit.

- To make the casings, fold the band in half lengthwise with wrong sides together. Pin and stitch the band to the right side of the skirt. Trim the seam to 3/8" and finish the edges.

- Stitch the first casing 3/8" from the top of the band and a second casing 3/8" below the first. This will form the third casing next to the skirt, slightly larger than the other two.

- Cut three pieces of elastic the length of your waist measurement plus seam allowances.

- Use a small safety pin to insert the elastic pieces into the casings. Then stitch the elastic ends together. I put a safety pin on both ends, so I can find the end easily if it slips into the band.

See also Waistbands.

Elastic

E

Embroidery

Q A recent article about François Lesage of Paris mentioned a crochet hook embroidery. How is this done?

A François Lesage is the master embroidery designer at Albert Lesage & Cie, perhaps the most important embroidery house in the world.

The crochet-hook technique used is tambouring, and it looks like a chain stitch. It is made with a tambour hook with a pointed end that penetrates the fabric. The background fabric is stretched taut on a large wooden frame, and the thread is held under the frame.

Tambouring is often used for attaching tiny beads which are already strung on fine thread. With the wrong side up, the tambour hook is used to crochet the thread between the beads. This is worked on a frame which can be flipped, so the design on the right side can be easily checked.

Two books with sections on tambouring are *Advanced Embroidery Techniques* by Beryl Johnson and *The Ladies' Guide to Needle Work* from R.L. Shep. (See Bibliography.)

Two articles on Lesage can be found in "Threads" in the April/May 1988 issue and in "Creative Needle" in the May/June 1988 issue.

Tambour hooks are available from Lacis (see Resource List).

Fabrics

Q What is ramie? Can you wash it? If so, does it shrink?

A Ramie or China grass, a stem fiber similar to flax, is grown in semitropical regions such as the Phillippines, China, Malaysia, and India. Until recently, it was used primarily for table linens.

The natural color of ramie is white or cream, but it dyes rapidly, with excellent absorbency and a high luster.

Ramie has now become more popular for wearing apparel. Pure ramie is washable. Shrinkage varies, since it is frequently blended with acrylics, cotton, wool, silk, and linen. Be certain to check the manufacturer's recommendations before washing.

Ramie table linens can be laundered like cotton or linen.

Q When I make skirts or blouses from cotton/polyester blends, they pill like acrylic sweaters after they've been washed. How can I prevent this?

A Pilling is a problem which cannot be prevented. However, pills can be removed with a twin-blade razor like an Atra® or Bic®. Take your time and scrape carefully.

Q I'd like to use a border print in a skirt, but I can't find a pattern. Can you help?

A Full dirndl skirts are perfect for border print fabrics. A dirndl can be made simply from a rectangle of fabric gathered onto a waistband; a pattern isn't really necessary, but you must plan carefully.

• Although the skirt can be any width around the bottom, most measure be-

F ᴏ̣ᴌ ᴏ̣ᴌ ᴏ̣ᴌ ᴏ̣ᴌ ᴏ̣ᴌ

Fabrics

tween 70" and 90". Be certain you buy enough fabric to fit around your hips, with lots of extra ease.

- The hemline is usually between 1/2" and 6" from the selvage. Decide where yours should be and pin it in place.

- To decide how long to make the skirt, "try on" the fabric. Pin the ends together at the center back, and, using tied elastic as a temporary waistband, shorten or lengthen the skirt until you find the look you like. Measure between the hemline and the elastic to determine your skirt length (see illustration).

- Determine the necessary width, adding the desired amount of ease for gathering.

- Add 5/8" seam allowances at the center back seam edges and the waist edge. Add your hem allowance (figured above). Record the final length and width in the margin of this page.

- Add 4" to your waist measurement to determine waistband length. This will give you a finished waistband 1" longer than your waist measurement, with two 5/8" seam allowances at the end and a 1-3/4" underlap. To determine the waistband width, double the desired finished width and add two 5/8" seam allowances.

- Unpin the fabric. Cut one waistband and one or two skirt rectangles using the measurements you calculated above.

- Sew the center back seam, insert a 7" skirt zipper, and gather the upper edge of the skirt to fit the waistband.

- Attach the waistband, positioning it so that the ends overlap. Generally, the front waistband is 1" longer than the back waistband.

- Hem the skirt to the desired length.

- Attach waistband hooks and eyes.

Elastic

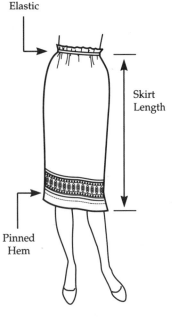

Skirt Length

Pinned Hem

Try on the fabric to determine skirt length.

Fabrics

Q Do ready-to-wear designers design special fabrics for their work or do they buy the same fabrics that we find in fabric stores?

A Some designers design their own fabrics, but most do not. However, since the ready-to-wear business is a $100 billion industry and the home-sewing market is a $4 billion industry, ready-to-wear designers have a much larger selection than do fabric retailers and home-sewers.

Find an excuse to go to New York, where you have a better chance of finding fabric outlets with ready-to-wear fabrics for sale.

See also Travel.

Q Why do you say that China silk cheapens a garment?

A Most China silks are very lightweight, plain weave fabrics which frequently don't have enough threads per inch to wear well.

To test, scrape your thumbnail across the fabric. If the threads separate, the fabric will slip and tear at stressed seams.

Even though China silk is an inexpensive silk fabric, it isn't cheap. For the same amount of money, you can purchase good-quality rayon linings like a crepe-backed satin or a firmly woven twill. Or, if you prefer a synthetic material, select one of the new breathable polyesters. I usually avoid polyester lining fabrics because they don't breathe or absorb moisture as well as the polyester blouse materials.

If you are making an important garment, follow the example of Yves Saint Laurent, who often uses silk charmeuse or crepe de chine in his haute couture collections.

F

Fabrics

Q Why do pattern companies always recommend more fabric than really needed?

A For several years, pattern layouts have been planned on computers. They're not only much more accurate than the old-fashioned manual layouts, but also much tighter, with less space between the pattern pieces.

All fabric requirements are figured to the *next* 1/8 yard, not to the *nearest* 1/8 yard. The layout that requires 3 yards 2" will indicate 3 1/8 yards, not 3 yards.

The computer, of course, does not know your special sewing needs. It has been programmed with specific but general information, not variables. That is, the fabric width is exact; the pattern is unaltered; the layout is simple; all seam and hem allowances will be cut exactly as indicated and all pieces will be cut out completely without any overlapping seam allowances.

You, however, probably do not fit the pattern perfectly. If you regularly have large amounts of fabric left, it is because:

- Your fabric is wider than the fabric width indicated for the layout. Even an inch makes a difference.
- You've altered the length or width of the pattern.
- You're not cutting all pattern sections for the same view. Perhaps you left off a pocket or chose a shorter sleeve length.
- You've allowed a smaller hem allowance.
- You've sometimes allowed one seam allowance to notch into another.
- You've refolded your fabric for several different pieces to save a few inches.

The only answer to purchasing *exactly* what you need is to plan your own layouts before

Fabrics

purchasing. If you use a pattern twice, this becomes easier. But to refigure yardage before you've made the pattern once can be time-consuming. This is why I recommend that dressmakers charge extra when their customers purchase less than the specific amount of fabric.

Q I have some cotton fabric from the early 1940s that I'd like to use in a quilt. I also have some Pendleton wool that's at least 15 years old. How old can a fabric be and still be usable?

A If your fabric appears to be in good condition and was of good quality in the first place, there's no reason it can't be used. The first sign of deterioration is fading; if there are any signs of fading, think twice about investing hours of labor into this project.

Be sure to hold the fabric up to a window or light to check for moth, cricket, or rat holes. If you find holes, dip washable fabrics in hot water (140 degrees or hotter) for ten seconds. This will destroy any larvae. Hang dryclean-only fabrics wrong side out in the sunlight for 15 to 30 minutes or send them to the drycleaners to be cleaned. This will kill moths or larvae in the fabric, but it won't protect the fabric from future attack. After the fabric has been treated, mark the holes carefully and cut around them.

Q I made a skirt from beautiful, silky crepe de chine. It was difficult to handle and now that I've finished, the left side seam bells out at the hemline. I'm afraid the skirt was cut off-grain. Can I correct this problem?

A If the garment was cut off-grain, the problem cannot be completely corrected;

Fabrics

however, you might be able to make it less noticeable.

First, determine if the left side of the skirt is actually off-grain. Thread trace the lengthwise grain at the skirt center and again 4" from the center. Thread trace the horizontal grain at the hipline and 10" below the hipline. Using a pencil, mark the same grainlines on the skirt pattern.

Pin the pattern over the skirt, matching the grainlines. If the skirt is on-grain, the seamlines should match.

If the skirt is off-grain, check to see whether it could be ripped, recut, and stitched with smaller seam allowances.

If the skirt is on-grain and the seamlines match, the problem arose during construction. Could the seamline or hem have been stretched where the skirt bells?

If the seamline was stretched, cut a piece of lining selvage the length of the pattern side seam. Then ease the skirt seamline to it. Stitch or hand sew and press.

If the hem allowance was stretched, try steaming to reshape it. Always test press on a scrap before using steam on a silk garment.

If the bottom of the skirt is stretched out of shape, rip out the hem and cut a piece of lining selvage the desired length. With the wrong side up, pin the selvage to the hemline, easing in the excess skirt fabric. Sew it in place permanently with a tiny running stitch. Press.

When laying out slippery fabrics, remember that an ounce of prevention is worth a pound of cure. Cover the cutting table with a flannel-backed, vinyl table cloth, so the flannel side is up. Lay out your fabric. Alternately, position the fabric carefully between a layer of tissue paper and the pattern pieces.

Fabrics

Pin and cut through all layers. I sometimes even stitch through all layers.

One final reminder: if a fabric is off-grain, *don't* purchase it. Although some sewing experts might disagree, I have found that it is almost impossible for home sewers to straighten the grain permanently. Theoretically, this should always be possible on natural fiber fabrics, but it isn't.

Q My client wants polyester doubleknit slacks. Where can I order this fabric?

A Several stores have limited selections. Write for swatches to (addresses in Resource List—charges usually refundable with subsequent order):

- Britex-by-Mail (swatches $5)
- G Street Fabrics (sample charts $10)
- Redlands Sewing Center (send large, self-addressed envelope with 65 cents postage)

See also Pants.

Q The edges on cotton knit fabrics curl while cutting and sewing. What can I do? Also, how should I handle hems on these fabrics, to avoid having them roll to the right side on the finished garment?

A The experts at Stretch & Sew offer the following tips for solving these problems:

- When cutting out, use weights to hold the pattern sections in place. Use ash trays, silver dinner knives, or cans of food, if you don't have regular fabric weights.
- Use a water-soluble glue stick to "baste" the seam edges together before stitching. Stitch on the seamline and again about 1/2" from the seamline to prevent rolling seam allowances on the finished garment.

F

Fabrics

- To avoid hems that roll, use a 1" to 1-1/2" hem allowance and fuse the hem in place with a fusible web like Stitch Witchery® before topstitching it.
- When hemming T-shirts that have a 5/8" hem, use a double needle to stitch the hem. Trim close to the stitched line.
- Cut a full 5/8" seam allowance instead of a 1/4" one when sewing cotton knits. Glue just the edges together and make a seam. Stitch again 1/4" from the seamline in the seam allowance. Trim close to the second stitched line.

See also Hems, T-shirts.

Q I'd like to make "tummy-control" slacks. Where can I find Lycra® spandex fabric?

A Because of the popularity of overlock machines (sergers), many sewing machine dealers and fabric stores are stocking two-way stretch materials suitable for "tummy-control" stays, swimsuits, and leotards.

If you can't find a suitable fabric in your area, write Kieffer's Lingerie Fabrics and Supplies for a catalog (see Resource List).

Q I purchased some foam-backed loopy fabric to make draperies. The foam flaked off into the feed dogs during sewing. I then tried stitching with the foam side up, but it wouldn't move through the presser foot. What do you suggest?

A This problem can occur with any sticky fabric and is easily solved by placing a piece of tissue paper under and above the fabric. When stitching with paper, always stitch with the paper grain so it will tear away easily. Determine the grain by tearing the paper lengthwise and again crosswise; it will tear straight and easily with the grain.

Q I gave up wearing polyester because it was so warm to wear. Now I'm hearing about a new kind of polyester. What is breathable polyester?

A Breathable polyester is a generic term indicating the fabric is relatively comfortable to wear in warm weather.

Polyester is normally a hydrophobic fiber, meaning it does not absorb moisture well. Greater absorbency means increased garment comfort.

Therefore, soil release and anti-static finishes are applied to polyester to improve the absorbency of the fabric, creating a breathable polyester.

To test a polyester before purchasing it, put a drop of water on a small swatch. If it spreads into the fabric, it will be more comfortable to wear than if it remains in a bead on top.

Q Can you tell me what is boiled wool, how is it made, and where can I find it?

A Boiled wool is wool fabric that has been dyed, knitted, and shrunk. The shrinking process felts the fabric, giving it a unique texture, allowing it to remain soft and flexible, as well as wind- and water-resistant. The original fabric was a 100% merino wool; however, many creative home sewers create boiled wools from other wools and fabrics they have knitted.

Geiger of Austria used boiled wool for years to make expensive ($120 to $300), unlined, braid-trimmed jackets. Recently it's become available to home sewers.

F

Fabrics

This easy-to-sew fabric doesn't ravel, so seam finishes are eliminated. It has enough body to maintain its shape without interfacing, and both sides look the same, eliminating the need for lining. It can be hand-washed and lasts almost forever.

If you are unable to find boiled wool in your local fabric store, order it from Classic Cloth (see Resource List). Send $5 (refundable with order) for swatches.

Fade Line

Q Last year I made a dark red, washable silk blouse. It now has a white line along the front fold. Is this a fade line and how can I prevent this in the future?

A Most silk fabrics are not as colorfast as synthetics, because dyes are applied to the yarn or fabric instead of being incorporated into the solution of the fiber. Dark colors—red, blue, purple, and black—tend to fade more quickly than light colors.

To reduce fading, dryclean. If you must hand wash, use cool water and add a little vinegar to the next-to-last rinse.

See also Creases.

Fit

Q How perfect does a garment have to be when it's home-sewn? I've made things that are not quite perfect and feel guilty wearing them (especially around other sewers), but the clothes I buy never fit and I wear them guilt-free.

A Garments don't have to be perfect to be wearable, attractive, or pleasure giving; however, you have to be comfortable wearing them. Most of my homesewing friends have much higher standards than my friends who purchase expensive ready-to-wear; they also tend to be bigger nit-pickers and more critical.

Use these guidelines to create an attractive custom-designed wardrobe that your sewing peers will admire.

Fit

- Sew easy-to-make designs and buy hard-to-sew garments.
- Know your sewing abilities and remember your time limitations every time you select a fabric and pattern.
- Let your fabric do the talking. Select simple styles with a minimum number of seams and details to showcase a beautiful fabric.
- Avoid more than one challenge in a garment.
- Don't combine difficult-to-sew fabrics with hard-to-fit or complicated designs.
- A less-than-perfect fit is better than a tired, overworked garment.
- Perfect your sewing skills by using each pattern for several garments and by using the same fabric for different designs.
- Experiment with different sewing techniques until you find the ones which work best for you.
- To save time and have more professional-looking garments, stitch them right the first time.
- Think success.

Q How do *you* check fit when you're sewing a new pattern?

A Depending on the design and fabric, I use one or more of the following to check a pattern's fit:

- My first choice is usually my basic sloper. Since the sloper is fitted, without any design ease, I know the new pattern can be no smaller than the sloper unless I'm sewing very close-fitting designs or stretchy fabrics.

F

Fit

- When my sloper isn't handy, I measure the paper pattern and compare the measurements to my body measurements plus wearing ease.
- I like pattern pin fitting, particularly when the design has a neckline that might be too revealing. Pin fitting is also a good way to check the garment length, so I can reduce the fabric requirement before cutting out.
- And when the fabric is unforgiving and ripping must be avoided, I make a test garment in muslin or nonwoven pattern cloth.

See also Bodice, Pants, Patterns

Fraying

Q I recently made a skirt from a wild silk fabric. To flatter my figure, I cut the garment on the crossgrain with the stripes running vertically, even though the fabric has a horizontal stripe. The garment is literally falling apart because of excessive fraying. Fray Check™ has not solved my problem, and I'm afraid sitting may cause the fabric to split. Can my skirt be salvaged?

A You may have to chalk this one up to a learning experience. But don't despair: everyone, even the most experienced designer, has an occasional disaster.

Your fabric has thick irregular threads in the filling (crossgrain) and small, smooth threads in the warp (lengthwise grain), so when cut on the crossgrain, seam slippage is a major problem.

You might be able to salvage the garment by underlining it with a firmly woven fabric like organza (silk or polyester). Take the skirt apart and underline each section, then reassemble the skirt. The underlining will support the stress and strain instead of the fashion fabric. However, excessive ripping and handling may be more than it can bear.

Here is another idea for salvaging the skirt. Using 1"-wide strips of lightweight fusible interfacing like Stacy's Easy Knit® or Armo's Whisper Weft, center and fuse over the vertical seam lines. To be sure the fusible won't add too much stiffness, try it on a fabric scrap before applying it to the garments. Also check for bleed-through or demarcation lines.

Most wild silks, tussahs, and shantungs won't hang or wear well when cut on the crossgrain. If you don't like horizontal stripes, either avoid these fabrics or consider this design idea, copied from expensive ready-to-wear. Cut half of the garment on the lengthwise grain and half on the crossgrain (see illustration). Be certain the garment has ample ease to avoid stress at the seams.

See also Seams.

Fraying

H

Hems

Q Every time I hem my jeans, I break the sewing-machine needle. What do you advise?

A Denim jeans aren't easy to hem and you aren't the only one with this problem. Denim is a very tightly woven fabric. When crossing seams, you are usually stitching through 12 fabric layers.

Use a sharp-pointed needle or use a Schmetz Jeans/Denim needle (size 100). Fold the hem in place and rub the stitching line with soap. Stitch. It might also help to use a needle lubricant. You can even pound the seam allowances with a hammer before stitching over them. This sounds a little crazy, but it softens the fibers, making them easier to penetrate.

Q Why do jeans hems roll to the right side (even on ready-to-wear) and how can I prevent it?

A The problem lies back at the factory. When they weave denim, it comes out askew, so they cut the jeans to compensate. Somehow this makes the hem roll to the right side. When you sew with denim, fuse the hem before topstitching it. For ready-to-wear, prepare to iron the hems each time you wash the jeans.

Q Is there any way to make skirt pleats hang closed at the hemline?

A To solve this problem, stay the fold line of the pleat using the selvage from a lightweight lining material, and use the Dior pleat finish to seam the pleats vertically.

• Determine the exact length of the fold line by measuring the pattern. Cut the stay 2"

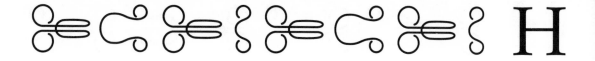
longer, mark the fold line length on it, and center the stay over the fold line.

- Carefully tack the stay in place to the wrong side of the skirt so the stitches won't show through. When using the Dior pleat finish, hem the skirt sections *before* the vertical seams are completed.

- Stitch the vertical seams, stopping 6" above the hemline. Then complete the waistband and closure.

- Try on the garment. Have a friend mark the hem length. Finish the hem edge and hem the garment.

- Starting at the hemline, complete the vertical seam lines.

- Trim and overcast the seam edges, either by hand or by machine.

Q When using a serger to make rolled hems on napkins, how do you keep the corners from raveling?

A Stitch continuously around three sides of the napkin. Then you only need worry about raveling on one corner. Thread the stitch chain at the fourth corner back into the stitches.

To turn corners, stitch to the fabric edge; take one more stitch off the fabric. Raise the needle and foot. With your right hand, pull the needle thread gently just above the eye of the needle. Then ease the threads off the stitch finger. Pivot the fabric, position the needle at the edge of the fabric, lower the foot, and continue stitching.

To fasten the threads at the end, I use a tapestry needle to thread the chain back into the stitches. Gale Hazen uses a tiny latch hook (like a knit picker) for this operation. For a quick and easy finish, use a fray retardant such as Fray Check™ or clear fingernail polish to prevent unraveling.

Hems

H

Hems

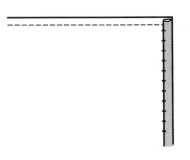

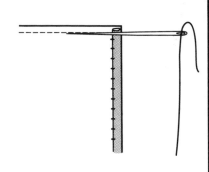

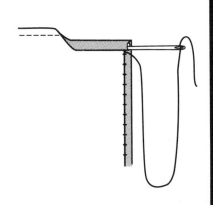

Q How do you handle a hand-rolled hem on the corners of scarves?

A It takes a little practice to hem corners smoothly. On a hand-rolled hem, the hem allowances overlap at the corners. The following directions are for right-handed sewers:

- Hem one edge to the corner. Then reposition the scarf so the next edge to be hemmed is held horizontally in your left hand with the wrong side toward you (see first illustration).
- Lay the needle along the unhemmed edge at the corner so the eye extends about 1" beyond the fabric (see second illustration).
- Roll the raw edge over the needle. Pull the needle out of the roll and hem the edge, working from right to left (see third illustration).

Here are some other suggestions for easier rolled hems:

- Place a line of machine stitching in the hem allowance 1/8" from the hemline. This stays the edge and provides a guide for making an even hem.
- Trim away the excess hem allowance 1/8" from the machine stitching. To prevent excess fraying, trim only 8" to 10" at a time.
- Dampen your left thumb and forefinger to roll a tight hem.
- Use a fine needle to hem the trimmed section with a slipstitch, felling stitch, or hemming stitch.
- Trim and hem until the edge is finished.

Q I frequently see blind-hemming machines listed in the used sewing-machine section of our paper at a cost of more than $300. What are they? If I bought one, would I use it often?

A A blind hemmer has only one thread and makes a chain stitch like the hems on ready-made garments.

The machine must be adjusted carefully to ensure invisible hemming stitches. This often takes more time than hand hemming and is therefore not practical for home sewers or those specializing in individual garments or alterations. However, this machine would be useful for small manufacturers who hem many identical garments.

Note: One of the pleasures of writing a column is the dialog through the mail with readers. After I answered the question above, several readers wrote to disagree with my opinion on the usefulness of blind hemmers for the home sewer. I am delighted that those of you with blind hemmers are having good results and consider the machine a good investment; I still feel, however, based on my teaching experiences, that most home sewers will not have equivalent results.

Your comments, whether you agree or disagree, are particularly important to me. Not infrequently they persuade me that another method or idea is better. I hope you will comment on this book, too. See the last page for more information.

Q Should the bottom edge of pant hems be straight across or should they dip in back? If the hem should dip, how much?

A The style and length of the pants will determine the shape of the hemline. Generally, classic, straight-legged pants and men's trousers extend at least to the top of

Hems

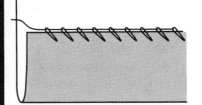

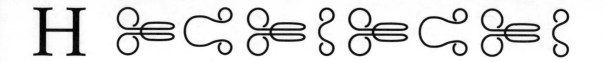
Hems

the instep or shoe in front. In back, the hem-line should extend at least to the middle of the shoe back, and some individuals prefer to have the back length reach the top of the shoe heel.

If the pants are hemmed straight across, there will be a deep break at the front of the pant leg. Although this is acceptable, some think it looks sloppy, as it breaks the line.

The break can be eliminated, or at least reduced, by shortening the pants in the front or by wearing a higher heel. The difference between the front and back lengths, the amount of the dip, is usually 1/2" to 3/4". On stove pipe pants, the difference may be greater than 1"; these designs will require a separate facing instead of a traditional hem.

Novelty pants, wide and narrow, which extend only to the ankle, rarely have a dip.

See also Pants.

Q A regular customer always asks me to hem his trousers 3/4" to 1" longer in back. Since the hems are usually 1-1/2" to 2" deep, I end up with excess hem in the back and not enough in the front. How can I achieve professional-looking results on this?

A A solution is to reduce the hem depth to 1-1/4"; however, men's pants hang better with a wide hem allowance. Also, if you can persuade your customer to accept a 1/2" slant, the hem will be easier to handle.

This method, used by tailors in expensive men's shops, differs from traditional home-sewing methods, yet it produces excellent results.

• Press the hem allowance to the wrong side.

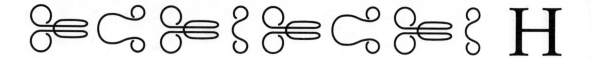

- At the center front, clip into the hem allowance 1/4" to 3/4". Treat the clipped edge with Fray Check™ and allow to dry.
- Pin or baste the hem in place, letting a small fold form at the center back.
- Hem the pants and press. The fold at the back should press flat and be inconspicuous. If it doesn't, secure it with a small stitch or two.

Most home sewers find these little folds objectionable and try all sorts of maneuvers to remove them. Since I've seen them on couture designs by Balenciaga and Dior, they're probably all right for us too.

Q How can I duplicate the narrow hems used on the prepleated dresses by Mary McFadden?

A One of my favorite narrow hems is the machine-rolled hem. Allow a 5/8" hem allowance.

- Machine stitch 1/2" from the cut edge.
- Fold the hem under on the stitched line and stitch close to the fold line, right side up (see first illustration).
- Use appliqué scissors to trim closely. Fold the hem again to the wrong side. With the wrong side up, stitch on top of the last row of stitching (see second illustration).
- For a decorative hem, set your machine on a medium width and length zigzag. You can use either matching or contrasting thread.

The secrets for making a quality narrow hem are to stitch as closely as possible to the fold line and to trim as closely as possible to the stitched line.

You can make larger ripples by experimenting with nylon monofilament thread in the

Hems

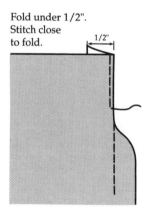

Fold under 1/2".
Stitch close
to fold.
1/2"

Fold hem again
and stitch.

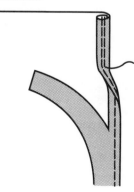

H

Hems

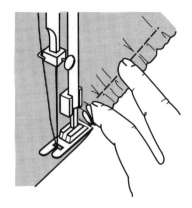

bobbin and/or needle, or by folding the hem over 20-pound fishing line.

Q I notice that you often advise us to crimp a hem. How do you do this?

A Hold your index finger firmly behind the presser foot as you stitch, so that the fabric pleats or forces more fabric into each stitch than usual. Stitch at 12 stitches per inch. This technique, also called ease-basting, will work well on almost every fabric (see illustration).

Q You've written that there isn't a foot for conventional sewing machines that makes a rolled hem. What do you mean? My machine comes with a rolled hemming foot.

A Let me clarify (my favorite verb). There isn't a foot for conventional sewing machines that will make a hem *that looks as if it were handrolled*. A hand-rolled hem is quite round and the stitches don't show. Though some machine hems are rounder than others, hems made with a hemming foot have stitches, whether straight or zigzag, that are always visible.

Q I've tried using a gathering stitch 3/8" from the edge to distribute ease evenly around the shirttail hems of bias skirts and around the curves of shirts—to no avail. I still get ripples. Why?

A Most purchased garments have considerably more ripple than the sample you enclosed. Eliminate ripples or drag lines in curved areas by basting with a washable glue-stick, water-soluble basting tape, or old-fashioned hand basting.

Interfacing

Q I've noticed that experts in articles and books always show more places interfaced than the patterns do. Why is this and how should I think through what needs to be interfaced on a garment (e.g., jackets)?

A Always consider the pattern only a guide. Remember that the pattern manufacturers cannot know your sewing skills, your criteria for the finished garment quality, your time available, or even the particular fabric you select. In addition, since they have a limited amount of space on the guide sheet, they can only provide you with some general guidelines.

Interfacings are the invisible ingredients that make garments a success. They support, preserve the garment's shape, add body and crispness, build unusual silhouettes, and prevent seam shadows.

When interfacing any garment, evaluate the garment design and fashion fabric. Will the fabric need the help of an interfacing to achieve the desired finished appearance? If so, decide where the interfacing will be needed and evaluate the characteristics of different interfacing materials to determine which will produce the desired result.

When interfacing a jacket, I always interface the collar, lapels, button/buttonhole area, pockets, and hems. If it is a winter jacket, I interface the upper back; if the fabric is too soft to remain smooth above the bust, I also interface there.

I

Interfacing

Q When I used Wonder-Under™ to fuse hems in the 1960s, they frequently came unfused after several launderings. You often recommend Wonder-Under™, so I bought some. Has the product changed?

A Yes. Although the name is the same, this isn't the same product. The only similarity is that Pellon manufactured both.

The new Wonder-Under™ is a fine, fusible web. Since holes in the web are miniscule, the permanent bond is solid and doesn't allow spots that won't fuse.

This paper-backed fusing agent can be used to make any fabric a fusible. Although it's used primarily for appliques and hemming, it has many other applications, including fuse-basting lapped seams on Ultrasuede®.

Q I often have trouble with fusible interfacings on cotton fabrics. I follow the directions, but the fabric still puckers or wrinkles where the interfacing is applied. What am I doing wrong?

A Cotton fabrics frequently wrinkle when you fuse interfacings to them with a press cloth that is too wet. This is because the fabric shrinks during the fusing process. Sometimes these wrinkles can be ironed away. If you continue to have problems, try one of the interfacings made by Armo. Use a dry press cloth and steam iron to fuse the interfacing to the fabric.

An alternative is to avoid fusibles on all-cotton fabrics; use sew-in interfacing.

Interfacing

Q I just can't seem to choose the right fusible interfacing for polyester crepe de chine and other polyester silky-type lightweight fabrics. What do you recommend?

A Since your letter didn't specify how much crispness you want or what kind of garments you are making, I'll assume you're making blouses and dresses and want to interface the cuffs, collars and front plackets in a way similar to better quality ready-to-wear.

I like knit and weft-insertion fusibles for lightweight silky fabrics. Be certain to pre-shrink them.

Purchase small amounts of several different interfacings and test them on your fabrics. Select the ones you like best and buy them in three- or five-yard lengths to have on hand whenever you need them. Be sure to ask for fusing directions when you make your purchases; the directions vary with each manufacturer.

I either store my interfacings in Ziploc® bags with the directions or if they come with instructions printed on plastic sheets, I sew up the sides of the plastic and store the interfacing inside.

Q I'm making a corduroy blazer and am wondering what kind of interfacing I should use. Also, how should I press the corduroy?

A A sew-in woven or non-woven interfacing is usually best for a blazer. Select a mediumweight interfacing unless the fabric is extremely lightweight or very heavy.

Fusibles can be used on some corduroys. Test by fusing the interfacing to a corduroy scrap to see if the nap becomes crushed during the

I

Interfacing

fusing process. Generally, it's better to apply fusibles to the facings instead of to the garment. To avoid a demarcation line when you must fuse the interfacing to the garment, pink all interfacing edges that won't be sewn into a seam.

Cover the ironing board with a thick terrycloth towel, a large scrap of your corduroy, or a Velvaboard® before fusing. Use a seam roll when pressing seams and darts to avoid impressions on the outside of the garment.

A good steaming on the right side is all that's necessary for most garments. Set the iron to steam and hold it just above the fabric, steaming the entire surface quickly. Use a stiff brush and brush with the nap, to further improve the look of the fabric.

Never allow the iron to touch the right side of the fabric. Use a cotton terrycloth press cloth or a corduroy fabric scrap to avoid crushing the nap. Place the cloth over the garment, with right sides together, and steam press with the nap.

Q My tailoring teacher insists that we avoid fusible and non-woven interfacings. I have read that you and others use fusibles for tailored jackets and think these interfacings are wonderful. Whom and what should I believe?

A This is one of the many personal choices you must make while sewing. Some fusible interfacings are excellent; however, it is extremely important to follow the manufacturer's instructions exactly.

Very expensive garments are made with fusibles. For example, I examined two Saint Laurent wool jackets recently. The $1,400 Rive Gauche design in ready-to-wear had only fusible interfacings. The $4,000 couture

Interfacing

jacket had a traditional hair canvas interfacing in the lapels, but fusibles in the cuffs.

Personally, I prefer woven sew-in interfacings or knit and weft- insertion fusibles to the non-woven types, but I sometimes use non-wovens, too.

Try a wide variety of interfacings. Then use the ones that give the results you want with the least amount of effort.

Sewing for yourself is a personal experience; you don't have to please anyone else. Some home sewers have more time and patience than others, as well as higher standards. Establish your own priorities and recognize your limitations; then use them as a guide every time you sew.

Q I'd like to duplicate the crisp collars on expensive men's dress shirts, using fusible interfacings. What do you recommend?

A This technique, inspired by an Yves Saint Laurent shirt, combines a woven sew-in interfacing and a fusible web to make smooth, stiff shirt collars.

The interfacings I like best are Pellon's Shapewell, Stacy's Veriform®, Armo-Press® Firm, and Formite II, but none is a fusible. However, with the use of a Teflon release sheet (Transfuse™ or Appliqué Pressing Sheet™) and a fusible web (Stitch Witchery®, Wonder-Under™, Transfuse™ II, Fine Fuse™), any fabric can be made fusible. (See Resource List.)

• Place the uncut interfacing on the pressing board with a slightly smaller piece of fusible web on top. Cover the interfacing and fusible with the Teflon release sheet. Press over the release sheet with the iron set on "wool" to fuse the layers together.

I

Interfacing

Let cool briefly; then remove the release sheet.
- Using the collar pattern, cut one interfacing section on the bias and one on the lengthwise grain; trim all edges 3/4".
- Fuse the bias-cut interfacing section to the wrong side of the upper collar. Then center and fuse the other interfacing section to the wrong side of the upper collar. Complete the collar. (*Note*: You understood correctly. Both interfacings are fused to the upper collar, one on top of the other. Neither is fused to the undercollar.)

See also Collars.

Q Can I use a knit fusible interfacing to line the front of an unlined jacket?

A Fusible knit interfacings are excellent underlinings for unlined jackets; but they can't be applied as lining.

Generally, if you underline an unlined jacket front, you should also underline the back so the garment will hang properly. I also recommend underlining the sleeves, so the jacket can be slipped on and off easily.

Using the front, back, and sleeve pattern pieces, cut out the underlining sections. Frequently the facings and hem allowances are underlined, but not always. This is a decision you'll have to make based on the fashion fabric, the underlining material, and the finished look you desire.

Fuse the underlining sections to the wrong side of the fashion fabric sections. Then assemble the garment.

Interfacing

Q I want to use fusible interfacing to give a suit jacket more body. What kind shall I use?

A Help! I need more information from you. Describe the fashion fabric. Is it a knit or woven? Light, medium, or heavy in weight? A synthetic, natural fiber or blend? Is it a soft, collarless design or a crisp, tailored jacket? Do you plan to line the garment?

For an unlined jacket, I frequently use a knit fusible like Stacy's Easy Knit® or Pellon's KnitShape™. It can be used on knits and wovens without appreciably changing the character of the fashion fabric. Most importantly, it is silky and allows you to slide into the jacket easily.

Some other fusible interfacings I like for underlining include Armo Weft, Whisper Weft, SRF™, and Fusible P-91, manufactured by Crown Textile Co., and Stacy's Suit-Shape®.

Based on the garment design, fashion fabric, and desired effect, I always experiment with several different interfacings, fusing them to fabric scraps before making a final decision. No fusible is right for every application; but with experimentation and the proper fusing techniques, you'll be assured success.

Q I'm frustrated! I use fusible knit interfacing in blouses. Then when I wash them, the interfaced areas bubble. What am I doing wrong and is it too late to fix?

A You *must* pre-shrink the knit fusible, even though they don't tell you to do so. It is shrinking at a different rate than the blouse fabric. All you can do now is use spray starch and hope no one notices. If you have extra fabric, sew new collar and cuffs.

I

Irons

Q What do you think of the new presses? What irons do you use?

A The new presses are fantastic for fusing, so if fusible interfacings and appliqués are an integral part of your sewing style, you will probably enjoy one; however, I do not feel a press is a substitute for a good iron.

I use a Sussman gravity flow iron. I also like the Naomoto iron, but these are expensive. If your budget can't withstand buying one, review the latest "Consumer Report" for the iron with the most steam.

See also Pressing.

Q My iron doesn't have a steam setting for synthetics or wools. When set for those fabrics, the iron releases water, not steam. How can I make steam without making the iron too hot for the fabric?

A When an iron is set on low or below the steam range, it isn't hot enough to make steam and it spits water.

Always test the effects of heat and moisture on fabric scraps before pressing or ironing. You frequently need more heat to set the seams and press the edges during the construction process than you need when the garment is completed.

Protect the fabric with a press cloth to avoid scorching, and don't hold the iron in one place too long. To prevent shines, press as much as possible from the wrong side and always use a press cloth when pressing from the right side.

Q Should I use a tailor's knot or a square knot to secure the end of a stitched line?

A The tailor's knot is a form of overhand knot. It will not loosen, once tied. It's better than the square knot because it's easier to position snugly at the end of a stitched line. A square knot may not hold securely when the threads are of different size.

- To make a tailor's knot, pull both threads through the fabric to the same side.
- Twist the ends together, loop them around your index finger, and pull the ends through the loop.
- Use your thumb or a pin to pull the knot snugly next to the fabric at the end of the stitched line.

Knots

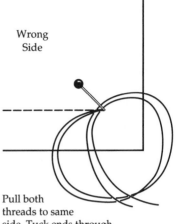

Wrong Side

Pull both threads to same side. Tuck ends through loop and pull snugly against fabric.

L

Lace

Q How do you mark darts on lace when it's an open-weave lace?

A Lay tape on the lace so you can mark the dart lines. On less open-weave lace, use pins with colored glass heads so they don't get lost.

Leather

Q I would like to make leather garments, but I don't want to spend a lot of money making mistakes while I learn. What do you suggest I make and where can I purchase leather and suede?

A Start with something simple like a belt or small handbag. Ghee's sells handbag patterns and findings, as does Jane Shaner.

Tandy Leather Co. has a variety of leather and suede. They have a video on sewing on leather and have also developed patterns for McCall Pattern Company. For a catalog, send $1.

Pigskin is available from Iowa Pigskin Sales Co. For swatches, send $4.

For more details on sewing on leather, consult my *Claire Shaeffer's Fabric Sewing Guide*.

See the Resource List for addresses.

Men, Sewing for

Q I have enjoyed sewing men's garments and love the well-tailored results, but I'd like a guide. Have you considered writing a book on tailoring for men?

A There is already an excellent book on this subject—*Classic Tailoring Techniques, A Construction Guide for Men's Wear*. Written by Roberto Cabrera and Patricia Flaherty Meyers, it is published by Fairchild Publications (see Bibliography). This comprehensive book has excellent sections on pattern adjustments, fitting, tailoring techniques, trouser construction, and alterations.

Q I have a small problem with my husband's favorite sport coat. The seamline joining the collar to the lapel has ripped out. Although this jacket is several years old, it was made by Hickey-Freeman and it wasn't cheap. How do I repair it so the mending won't show? Is this going to happen again?

A The gorge line or seamline which you describe was finished by hand with mercerized cotton thread. In time, the thread may break and cause the seam to unravel. This hand finish is a sign of a quality garment and is very easy to repair.

Realign the seamline, matching the folded edges. Then baste through the collar section about 1/4" above the seamline and the lapel section about 1/4" below the seamline. Use a small ladder stitch to sew the gorge line permanently. To make the stitches invisible, sew through the sides of the folds rather than through the top. Be sure the stitches are parallel to each other and don't slant.

Don't reserve this technique only for repairs. It can also be used for garment assembly.

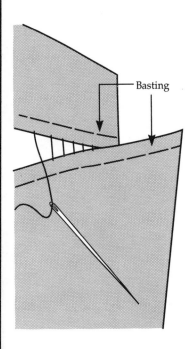
Basting

Men, Sewing for

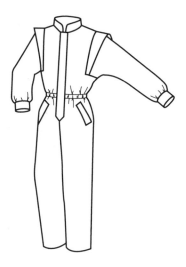

Q I am looking for a man's jumpsuit pattern. Where can I buy one?

A Try the Black Butte Jumpsuit from Green Pepper (#142). For variety, use his favorite shirt patterns to redesign the top of this multisized pattern.

See the Resource List for address.

Q I love to sew for my husband, but I have trouble finding patterns, fabrics, and tailoring supplies. Can you help?

A You have two choices: buy an existing pattern, of which there are not a lot of sources; or have a pattern custom-made, either by yourself or by someone else.

Various classic men's designs are offered by Kwik-Sew and by Stretch & Sew Patterns, available in many fabric stores. You might also investigate Daisy Kingdom, Designer Jeans, Donner Designs, Green Pepper, Jean Hardy Pattern Co., and Sew Easy for active sportswear, western, and outdoor designs for men.

The catalogs from Folkwear, Fashion Blueprints, and Pauloa Patterns include traditional, folk, and ethnic designs for men. Patterns for historical designs are available from Past Patterns.

Your best source for custom patterns may be Tailor-Craft, which specializes in custom designs for men.

If you want to draft a pattern yourself, here are some excellent books (see the Bibliography for annotations):

- *Modern Garment Design and Grading Clothing for Men and Boys*, by Master Designer includes how to adjust for figure variations.

- *Fundamentals of Men's Fashion Design: A Guide to Tailored Clothes* by Masaaki Kawashima; *Fundamentals of Men's Fashion Design: A Guide to Casual Clothes* by Edmund B. Roberts; and *Men's Outerwear Design* by Masaaki Kawashima are easy-to-read textbooks published by Fairchild Publications. They should be available through your library loan service.

- I've already mentioned another book published by Fairchild—*Classic Tailoring Techniques: A Construction Guide for Men's Wear* by Cabrera and Meyers. It includes a wealth of information on classic tailoring techniques, trouser construction, fitting, and altering menswear.

As for tailoring supplies (hymo, linen, pocketing and selisia, linings, wigan, and zippers), order from Oregon Tailor Supply Co.

Q Where can I buy a man's shirt pattern in a size 17 1/2 or 18? What should I do if it isn't large enough around the tummy?

A Kwik-Sew 662 (size 48-50) is the answer to your problem. It's a pattern for a dress shirt with a back yoke, two-piece collar, tab placket, and long or short sleeves. The shirt back has an optional pleat at the yokeline which will allow a little more ease through the body of the shirt.

Kwik-Sew sells a variety of king-sized patterns. Although some of them may be too tapered to fit around your husband's waist, this is easy to change. Just straighten the side seam by redrawing it to make it parallel to the center front (see illustration).

See also Alterations, Books, Collars.

Men, Sewing for

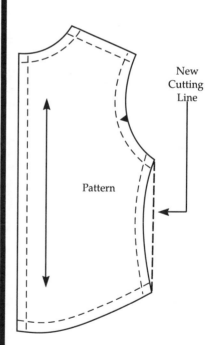

New Cutting Line

Pattern

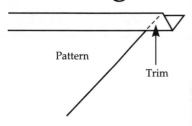
Open Chain   Open Chain

Mitering

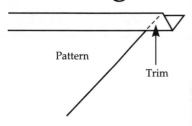

Pattern

Trim

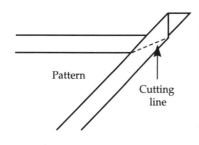

Pattern

Cutting
line

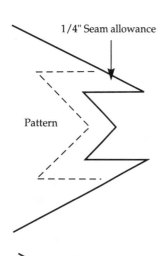

1/4" Seam allowance

Pattern

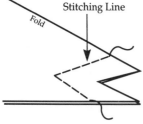

Stitching Line

Fold

Q How do you miter the corners on triangular scarves?

A Use the following method for a double-fold miter on any shape of corner.

- Make a paper pattern duplicating the corner angle (see first illustration).
- Fold each hem twice exactly as it will be sewn.
- Draw and cut a line from the point where the hems meet to the point of the scarf (see second illustration).
- Open the pattern out and add 1/4" seam allowances (see third illustration).
- Using the pattern, cut out the corners of the scarf. With right sides together, stitch a 1/4" seam (see fourth illustration).
- Trim the seam allowance. Turn the scarf right side out and hem.

See also Collars.

Needles

Q What is a wing needle and how is it used?

A A wing needle (sometimes called a hemstitching needle) can be used on most sewing machines. This large, oval-shaped needle works like an awl and makes small holes in the fabric when you stitch. It is often used in machine heirloom sewing (sometimes called French handsewing by machine), in combination with laces, entredeux, pintucks, and decorative stitches.

On most machines, the key to good results with a wing needle is to select a stitch pattern that allows the needle to stitch into some holes several times. This enlarges the holes and makes them more noticeable.

If you have a computer machine, you will be able to fine-tune your stitches on a sample, so that the wing needle hits each hole the second time exactly where it originally made the hole, without splitting any threads. Be certain that you use the size wing needle recommended for your machine. If you use one too large, you could damage the machine.

One computer machine has exceptional capabilities for machine heirloom sewing: the Elna 7000. Its stitches are designed to give hemstitching results without using a wing needle. For more information on techniques, consult *Know Your Elna* by Jackie Dodson and Carol Ahles (see Bibliography).

Carol Ahles tells me the best fabrics for this type of stitching are closely woven (sheer or lightweight), all-natural fabrics. Swiss cotton batiste, Swiss organdy, and handkerchief linen are the classic choices.

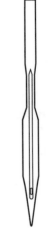

Needle Hole

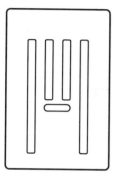

Zigzag
plate

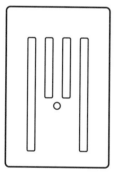

Straight
stitch
plate

Q My zigzag machine has a wide needle hole. I think I would get better results on some fabrics if the hole were smaller. Is there a way to change this?

A There's no question you'll have better results and fewer stitching problems when straight stitching on some fabrics if you would use a single-hole or straight-stitch needle plate.

Check with your dealer to learn if one is available for your machine. Also check the catalog from Sewing Emporium (see Resource List). Otherwise, try one of the following ideas:

- Use a straight stitch foot or any other foot which will hold your fabric more firmly than the all-purpose zigzag. I sometimes use the jeans foot on my Bernina.

- Depending on your brand of machine, reposition the needle to the extreme right or left of the zigzag hole and test the results. One or the other will put the needle closer to the bobbin hook and lessen the chances of the needle dragging the fabric down into the hole.

- Use tissue paper or a stabilizer such as water-soluble, Trace Erase™, Tear Away™, or Stitch-N-Tear™ between the fabric and the machine bed.

- Cover the needle hole with transparent tape. Make a hole in the tape by turning the handwheel manually two or three times, using an unthreaded needle.

- Take your needle plate off and set it on a 3x5 index card. Trace the openings for the feed dogs and needle. Cut out the feed-dog openings with an X-acto knife or scissors. Replace the needle plate. Tape the card in place over the needle plate. Now make a hole in the card with an unthreaded needle.

See also Seams.

Pants

Q I have trouble fitting slacks for a customer who has very slim thighs and a protruding stomach and seat. When the pants fit over the stomach and hips, she has too much fullness in the front crotch area. When I try to remove the fullness in the thighs, smile lines appear. Can you rescue me?

A The smile lines indicate that there isn't enough fabric. Although this will occur when the width of the pants' front is too narrow, it is probably because the crotch length needs to be extended at the inseam (see illustration).

Pants Fit For Your Figure by Louise Bame is a comprehensive guide to fitting pants patterns. The Bame Method includes point-by-point pattern adjustments, as well as suggestions on how to evaluate and correct the test garment.

I also like Leonora Johnson's pattern, available from Tacony. This is purchased according to the fullest hip measurement. The test garment is sewn first, then fitted to your body.

Clothing Design Concepts, Inc. offers an individualized pants pattern developed by home economist Laura Varney. The pattern is made on a computer using an individual's exact measurements. It is guaranteed to fit.

Ruth Oblander of Sew/Fit recommends that you buy a commercial pants pattern two sizes smaller than the hip measurement (but buy enough fabric for the actual hip measurement). Then the pants will be more likely to fit nicely through the legs and you can alter for the larger waist and hips.

Don't forget to help clients choose designs that will fit them attractively. You can make any garment fit an unusual figure, but that will not guarantee the design's suitability for that figure.

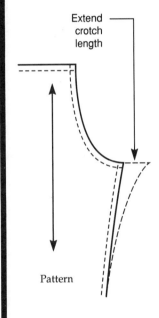

Extend crotch length

Pattern

P

Pants

Q The pants I made of polyester gabardine just keep getting longer and longer. When my Sew/Fit instructor suggested I test the stretch. I discovered there was stretch in the lengthwise grain but not the crossgrain. I then made another pair of pants on the crossgrain so the stretch would go around. Does this happen often in fabrics? Should I be checking for this?

A I haven't encountered this problem with regular gabardines—polyester, silk, or wool. However, fabrics can be woven with stretch yarns in the warp (lengthwise grain), as well as in the filling (crosswise grain) or in both (two-way stretch).

Generally, garments are cut so the stretch goes around the body. Ski pants and unitards are exceptions. When working with stretch fabrics, consider the garment use and design before cutting.

I am concerned that the fabric continues to grow, indicating that the fabric did not have good recovery. Perhaps you bought a novelty fabric from a manufacturer's cutting room.

It usually isn't necessary to check fabric stretch except when using a pattern designed exclusively for stretch fabrics.

Q Lots of my customers need alterations for a "dropped derriere." What do you suggest?

A Restitch the back crotch seamline as shown. The individual figure will determine how much you need to lower the new seamline. Lower the seam 1/8" at a time, trimming to the old stitching, until the pants fit. This alteration can be done on ready-to-wear, as well as on the pants you sew.

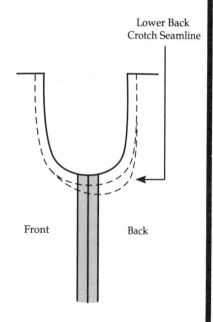

Lower Back
Crotch Seamline

Front   Back

P

Q How do you narrow the legs on slacks? I know this isn't hard, but I don't know exactly how to do it.

A Pants are usually narrowed from the knee down; however, if your legs are unusually thin or the pants are unusually wide, begin narrowing about mid-thigh.

Turn the pants wrong side out. Take out the hem. Press the seam allowances and hem flat. Pin new stitching lines for the inseams and outseams, narrowing each leg an equal amount at the hemline. Turn the pants right side out and try them on. If you like what you see, you're ready to sew; if not, repin and try again.

See also Fabrics, Fit, Hems.

Pants

Q What pattern styles and fabric designs are flattering to a short person with a large bust?

A Select V-necklines, small-scale prints and plaids, vertical lines or stripes, and monochromatic color schemes. For a comprehensive treatment of this subject, consult the terrific book *Short Chic* by Allison Kyle Leopold and Anne Marie Cloutier (see Bibliography).

This book is filled with inspiration and innovative ideas for dressing tall when you're actually short. It includes excellent hints for alterations and sewing.

As with most of the books I recommend, it is available from your local library.

Patterns

P

Patterns

Q I'd like to take apart a favorite pair of shorts to use as a pattern. How do you lay out the pattern to make sure it is straight on the grain?

A First, mark the shorts carefully on both the crossgrain and lengthwise grain. (If you're copying a dress, coat, or slacks, mark both grainlines in several places.) Usually, you mark with a thread tracing on the outside of the garment; however, if you're planning to trace the pattern immediately after marking the grainlines, it's faster to use an air-soluble marking pen.

If the garment is made of a woven stripe or plaid, follow the pattern in the fabric to mark the grainlines. If the grainline is difficult to locate, as in twill weaves and napped fabrics, try working from the wrong side. If you don't plan to wear the garment again, mark the grainlines with a soft-lead pencil. To save time and to avoid frustration when marking grainlines, use a lighted magnifying glass.

After marking grainlines on each piece of the garment, use the actual garment pieces as you would a paper pattern, aligning grainlines as you pin it to the new fabric and adding seam allowances where necessary.

If you prefer to make a pattern from the finished garment without taking it apart, use the following method:

- Purchase non-woven patternmaking cloth like Pellon® Tru-Grid™, which has a printed, 1"-square grid, making it unnecessary to mark grainlines on the new pattern. Another product is Staple Sewing Aids' Pattern Tracing Cloth, which is printed with a 1"-square dotted grid that also acts as a grainline guide.

- Mark the grainlines on the garment as described earlier.

- Working with one garment section at a time, pin a piece of the patternmaking cloth on top of the garment, matching the garment grainlines with the grid lines.

- If the section has a dart, smooth and pin the pattern cloth carefully toward each side of the dart until the pattern cloth stands up on top of the dart line (see illustration). Pin the dart in place.
- Use a soft lead pencil to trace the seamlines, dart lines, and the point of the dart onto the patternmaking cloth. Add generous seam and hem allowances.
- Remove the pattern cloth from the garment. Cut it out, pin it together, and try on the pattern. Make any necessary adjustments.

Q I have lost a lot of weight. I'd like to sew a new wardrobe, using some favorite patterns, but many are no longer available. How can I grade a pattern down from a size 16 to a size 12?

A Congratulations! Losing the weight was probably more difficult than grading the patterns will be. Grading isn't hard, but it does take time and should be done carefully. To ensure accuracy, grade only one size at a time. First, grade from size 16 to size 14. Then grade from a size 14 to a size 12.

Survey your patterns carefully before grading. Will you like them as well as on your new figure? Are they still fashionable? Perhaps you'd like a complete change.

I cannot teach you to grade in this short space. I recommend you consult *Grading Women's and Misses Garment Design* by M. Rohr, *ABC's of Grading* by M. Scheier, and *Grading Techniques for Modern Designing* by Price and Zamkoff (see Bibliography for annotations). They are available from the FIT Bookstore (see Resource List).

Patterns

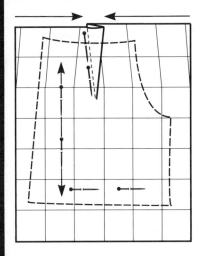

P

Patterns

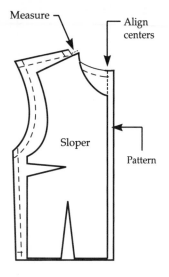

Measure

Align centers

Sloper

Pattern

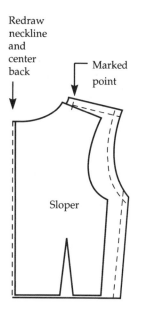

Redraw neckline and center back

Marked point

Sloper

Q Once you've made a sloper, how do you use it to check patterns?

A One of the advantages of making a sloper is that you get to know your body intimately and you understand how your body deviates from the perfect figure. This knowledge alone will help you when sewing your designs.

Let me tell you about my body irregularities and how they influence my pattern size, as well as when and where I adjust. I have a wide back neck, large waist and hips for my bodice size, and short arms and legs. When sewing skirts and slacks, I purchase a larger size pattern so that I have fewer fitting problems. When sewing suits, this isn't possible, so I fit the top and adjust the bottom, using either a pivot or a slash method. When sewing tops, I always use my sloper because I know the pattern must be widened 1/2" to 1" at the center back before cutting or the garment will never fit properly. The design of the sleeve determines when and if I shorten the sleeve, but I always shorten slacks before cutting.

When using a sloper, start with an area that usually fits to determine how the design deviates from the sloper. Once you know how or where it's supposed to fit, your sloper will show you where to make changes.

Here's how I use my sloper to adjust for a wide back neck. I start with the front sloper and bodice front. With the garment centers aligned, I move the sloper up until it meets the neck point on the shoulder seam; then I measure the distance between the neck points on the pattern and the sloper. I mark that distance on the shoulder seam of the sloper back (see first illustration).

Now I'm ready to adjust the garment back pattern. With garment centers parallel, I align the marked point on the sloper back and the neck point on the garment pattern. I trace the center back of my sloper to redraw the center back seam or foldline on the pattern (see second illustration). I adjust facings, trims, or collars accordingly, so they can be sewn to the garment neckline smoothly.

See also Fit.

Patterns

Q I've bought several pieces of fabric with diagonal design, but I'm having trouble finding suitable patterns for them. Have you seen any patterns I can use?

A Since diagonal designs and twill weaves cannot be matched at the seamlines, most patterns include special warnings that these fabrics are not suitable. Some styles, such as blazers, gored skirts, and bias-cut designs cannot be cut attractively, but many patterns can be used to create stunning outfits.

When used for clothing, diagonals should not chevron. They should progress around the body, slanting consistently in one direction. This affects the way set-in sleeves look when the garment is viewed from the front or back. Even though the piece might have been cut correctly, many home sewers find the look offensive (see illustration).

Simple styles with straight, rather than shaped seams are best. Diagonal designs are suitable for cardigan jackets, straight skirts, dirndls, and slim-fitting sleeveless dresses. Avoid bias-cut seams, kimono sleeves, gored skirts and collars. Or use plain contrasting fabrics for collars, pocket flaps, and other add-on details.

Fabrics with diagonal designs do not usually require with-nap layouts.

The best way to determine what you like and dislike about fabrics with diagonal designs is to go shopping for ideas. Start in the men's

P

Patterns

department, where you'll find many twill (a diagonal weave) jackets. Also watch for ideas in fashion magazines. Clip them and store them in this book, for further use and inspiration.

Q I've been hearing a lot about Burda patterns. Are they printed in English? Do they have a seam allowance? Are they only for experienced home sewers?

A Burda patterns are sold in 18 countries; hence, all instructions are printed in English, as well as in German and French. Measurements are given in inches and centimeters, like patterns from major American companies.

Burda patterns are multi-sized and do not include seam or hem allowances. These features make the patterns easier to adjust, but can make them more time-consuming to cut.

Seam and hem allowances can be marked with a double tracing wheel or with a tape measure. The secret to using the latter is to select a tape measure that is exactly 5/8" wide. You may prefer to invest in an Olfa Rotary Cutter (RTY-3) with a guide that can be set for the desired width; while the guide moves along the seamline, the cutter does its job on the unmarked cutting line.

It is important to know your body measurements and to use the size chart in the back of the pattern book, as Burda patterns do not have a lot of design ease. The size chart is fantastic. It includes the front waist length, back width, shoulder and sleeve lengths, neck and upper arm width, as well as the basic measurements—bust, waist, hips, and back-waist length.

The guide sheets are well-written, nicely illustrated, and feature techniques which enable you to produce professional-looking

Patterns

garments; however, they're a little more difficult for novices to use. Burda offers a toll-free number (800-241-6887) for help with sewing problems or to locate your nearest dealer.

Q I'd like to design my own clothes and make my own patterns. Can you recommend books on this subject?

A Although there are approximately 25 books on pattern drafting and patternmaking available, I don't know of a how-to book on fashion design that's in print.

Of the 25 books available, most include only technical details for drafting the basic sloper (shell) and making patterns. They do not address fashion design.

All of the following are well-illustrated, have up-to-date information, and can be borrowed from the library. (See Bibliography for annotations.)

- *Designing Apparel Through the Flat Pattern* by Kopp, Rolfo, Zelin, and Gross and *Basic Pattern Skills for Fashion Design* by Bernard Zamkoff and Jeanne Price were written by faculty at the Fashion Institute of Technology in New York City and are textbooks for those students who want to work in the fashion industry.

- *Professional Patternmaking for Designers: Women's Wear, Men's Casual Wear* by Jack Handford is also written for aspiring designers. In addition to patternmaking basics for women's wear, it includes how to draft basic slopers and some designs for men.

- *Pattern Making by the Flat-Pattern Method* by Norma Hollen is used in many home economics programs. Patternmaking techniques are applied to a commercial pattern sloper like Vogue 1004.

P

Patterns

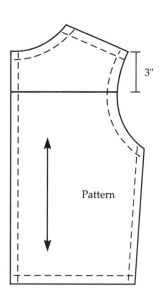

Pattern

3"

- *Patternmaking for Fashion Design* by Helen Joseph Armstrong is the most complete patternmaking book for women's designs. It also includes how to draft basic slopers and has an index.

Q I have osteoporosis. Although I've read everything I could find on pattern adjustments for this problem, I've never found one that addresses a severely rounded (see first illustration) back. Can you help?

A For best results, you'll have to experiment; no book can prescribe an alteration for all people with this problem. However, I've found that a key to fitting this figure is to add a seam at the center back if the pattern doesn't have one.

Before you begin working, practice by shaping a muslin square to fit your pressing ham. This exercise will help you understand how a two-dimensional fabric is darted or seamed to fit a three-dimensional body.

Trace the pattern back and cut out the new pattern. Place it on a large sheet of tissue paper. Draw a line at right angles to the center back about 3" below the neckline (see second illustration). Cut on the horizontal line. If the garment has a shoulder dart, slash through the center of the back shoulder almost but not quite to the horizontal line (see third illustration). If the garment does not have a shoulder dart, slash through the center of the back shoulder seam almost but not quite to the horizontal line.

Have someone measure your center back from the neck to the waist. On the slashed pattern, spread the center back as much as needed to equal the measurement you just made.

Spread the shoulder seam dart 3/4"-1" and tape to the tissue paper (see third illustration).

If the line of the center back isn't straight after all these adjustments, draw a smooth curve and add a seam allowance at the center back (see third illustration).

Now test the pattern in muslin. Mark the crossgrain 5" below the neckline and the lengthwise grain about 2" from the center back. When fitting, the crossgrain should remain horizontal and the lengthwise grain should be perpendicular to the floor. Pin the new dart at the back shoulder seam, so it fits the body smoothly. It should point toward the fullest part of the shoulder blade, ending about 2" short of the fullest part. If the dart is wider than 1" at the shoulder seamline, consider easing the excess into the seamline.

Although additional shaping can be obtained by adding a second dart from the neckline seam, this adds an unprofessional look to the garment.

Remove the muslin from the figure. Redraw the armscye curve if it has become distorted. Fold the dart as it will be stitched and correct the shoulder seam line.

Designer Balenciaga recognized many of his customers had rounded backs, and he lowered the back neckline to flatter this figure irregularity.

See also Fabrics.

Q I am a dressmaker and some of my customers are quite small, so I need adult patterns in sizes 3 to 7. As pattern grading is tedious, what are the alternatives?

A The Kwik-Sew and Stretch & Sew pattern companies have a larger size range than some of the other pattern companies, but the styles are limited. You can order some Vogue patterns in small sizes; see the back of the pattern book for information.

Patterns

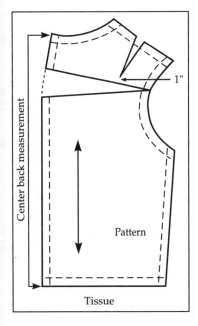

Center back measurement

1"

Pattern

Tissue

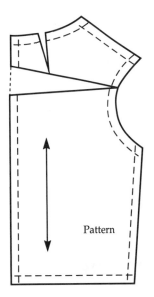

Pattern

Patterns

Sew/Fit sells an overlay pattern for sizes 1, 2, 3, and 4, available through their counselors. The overlay can also be ordered from Fit For You (see Resource List).

Q Why is a size 14 pattern so much larger than a ready-to-wear size 14?

A Pattern sizes have never been the same as ready-to-wear sizes. In truth, pattern sizes are much more reliable than ready-made garments, because all the major companies use the same set of standardized body measurements as their base.

In the fashion industry, standards regarding sizing don't exist. Sizing is arbitrary and varies with the manufacturer and the garment. In fact, sizing is more frequently related to vanity and price than garment size—the higher the cost, the larger the garment and the smaller the size.

Figure Types and Size Ranges by Debbie Ann Gioello and Beverly Berke defines a variety of body types and lists key body measurements, not garment measurements, for the various sizes. The book includes both the standard measurements frequently used by the Mail-Order Association of America and the measurements used by the pattern industry. If you can't get this book through your local library, order it from Fairchild Publications (see Bibliography).

Piping

Q When I stitch the cord into bias strips for piping, the fabric ripples. Would the purchase of a braiding foot help? Will the ripple disappear when the piping is sewn into a pillow?

A Corded piping often ripples if the strips are not cut precisely on the bias. The secret is to mark the cutting lines *exactly* on the bias; then cut with scissors or a rotary cutter. (See illustration for Bias.)

Also, the under layer of the bias strip may be creeping as you stitch. To prevent this, hold the strip firmly in front and back of the foot. If the creeping persists, use a washable glue stick to baste the layers together. You can also stitch over a strip of fabric stabilizer, such as Pellon's Stitch-n-Tear™, Tear Away, or Stacy's Appli-Quik™.

The rippling will not disappear when the cording is applied. In fact, it frequently gets worse.

The braiding foot you mentioned is designed for applying decorative cords and braids to the right side of a garment. For corded pipings, I recommend an adjustable zipper foot. This foot can be used to make cording with big, fat cords as easily as with small ones. Since it is adjustable, it allows you to position the first row of stitching farthest from the cord and the last row—the seamline—closest. This technique eliminates unwanted stitching lines on the finished garment between the seam and cording.

Some brands of machines have special feet to help apply piping—e.g., Bernina's bulky overlock foot, Viking's piping foot, etc. Check with your local dealer, write the mail-order companies in the Resource List who specialize in machine accessories, or read Chilton's *Know Your Sewing Machine* series (with machine-specific books for Bernina, Elna, New Home, Pfaff, Singer, Viking, and White). (See the Bibliography.)

Piping

Piping

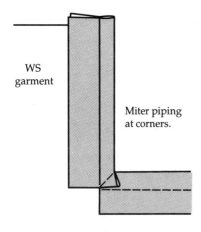

WS
garment

Miter piping
at corners.

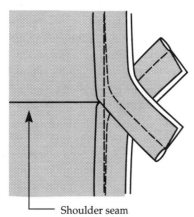

Shoulder seam

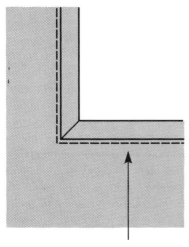

Topstitch through
all layers.

Q I recently tried to face a square neckline with piping. It was a disaster: the corners wrinkle and the ends of the piping meet unattractively. How can I get a professional finish next time?

A For easier, smoother application, reinforce each neckline corner before stitching the piping to the garment. Use a short stitch and stitch very close to the seam line for 1" on each side of the corner. Then clip to the stitched line.

If the piping is corded, a small wrinkle will always occur at the corners. If the piping is flat or uncorded, miter it on the underside at each corner using a hand or machine stitch (see first illustration).

The best and least conspicuous way to join the two ends is to seam them together before applying the piping. Measure the seam line around the garment neck; then measure and mark an equal length on the piping stitching line. Rip the piping apart as needed, so the ends can be joined together on the lengthwise grain. Restitch the piping as needed, center the joint seam over the left shoulder, and set the piping to the neckline.

An easier way to finish the ends is to begin stitching the piping to the neckline on the back, 1" below the left shoulder, leaving a piping tail 2" long. Continue around the neckline and stop 2" before the starting point. Lap the ends so the raw edges extend beyond the raw edge of the garment (see second illustration). Stitch the piping in place and trim the ends.

Piping may also be used as a facing. Finish the neckline by folding and pressing the seam allowances to the inside of the garment. Then topstitch through all layers immediately below the seam line (see last illustration).

P

Because clipped corners of square necklines tend to fray, I usually cover them with a shaped facing before topstitching.

Q I want to use my ruffler foot to make yards of ruffles. What formula should I use to determine the length of fabric I need to end up with a specific length of ruffles?

A The amount of fullness is determined by the type and grain of the fabric, the stitch length, and the ruffler settings. Therefore, I cannot give you one set formula.

To accurately determine the required length, make a sample.

- Cut a strip one yard long on the intended grain of the finished project.
- Set the ruffler according to the instruction manual. Working on a scrap, adjust the stitch length to produce the desired look. Remember: shorter stitches make fuller ruffles.
- Insert your one-yard fabric strip and stitch.
- To determine how many ruffled inches a one-yard strip will make, measure the stitched line. Record this information, as well as the stitch length and the ruffler setting.
- Measure all of the edges of your project where you plan to attach ruffles. To calculate how many yards of fabric strips you'll need, divide the total project length by the finished length of your ruffled strip. Round up to the next yard for safety and then add an extra yard to be sure you won't be caught short. For example, if your one-yard ruffle became 12" ruffled and the lower edge of your skirt measures 144", you need 12 yards of pre-ruffled fabric. Add an extra yard for a total of 13 yards of strips. Before ruffling, seam pieces together and hem if needed.

Piping

Presser Feet

P

Presser Feet

Q How do you use the rolled hemmer foot on shirttail curves?

A For shirttails, I prefer a machine-rolled hem to a rolled hemmer foot. When using a rolled hemmer foot, curved hems are difficult to stitch without drag lines; vertical seams won't feed through the foot smoothly; and for most homesewers, it's not worth the time it takes to master the foot.

David Coffin, Assistant Editor at "Threads" and author of *The Custom Shirt Book,* disagrees and uses a hemming foot whenever possible. Sometimes he recuts the hem to get a gentler curve. He also admits that some wrinkles come with the territory.

When using the foot, crimp the hem 1/2" from the raw edge. Then trim close to the crimped line. Try to avoid cutting the long threads at each end, so you can use them to thread the fabric into the spiral of the foot. With the raw edge held perpendicular to the sewing table, hem the edge.

David recommends that you stitch to the side seam, stop and skip over it, and then start again. Finish the unstitched section with regular machine stitching.

Gail Brown has a neat trick for starting the fabric into the spiral. She stitches a small piece of water-soluble stabilizer to the beginning of the fabric and trims it even with the edge to be rolled. She begins stitching on the stabilizer, rolling it into the foot. By the time you reach the real fabric, the edge is rolling nicely. Later, you can dissolve the stabilizer.

See also Hems.

Pressing

Q I work in a bridal shop and we sell many expensive dresses and gowns. We have problems pressing taffeta, chiffon, and crepe dresses. They often stretch out of shape when they are pressed. Even with special attention, it still happens. How can we prevent this?

A Without knowing more about your situation, it is difficult to solve your particular problem; however, here are some general rules for pressing gowns:

- Place a cardtable or chair under the end of the ironing board, so the garment doesn't hang off the board and stretch.
- Press; don't iron. Remember, pressing requires an up- and-down motion. Ironing is a sliding motion. Lots of us iron when we should really be pressing. If you are sliding the iron, be sure it is with the grain, not along the bias of the fabric. This is particularly important with flared skirts on bridal gowns.
- Try a Steamstress® instead of an iron. Most dresses need only a light kiss of steam.
- Use a presscloth. You will be less likely to press the dress out of shape.
- When all else fails, take the dresses to a good drycleaner for final pressing. They are better equipped than most alteration workshops.

See also Weddings.

Q How can I achieve a more professional look when pressing woolens and poly-gabardine garments? Ready-to-wear garments have a crispness that I haven't been able to achieve.

A Synthetic fabrics and some woolens have a springy quality that makes them very difficult to press crisply. It can be done, but

P

Pressing

you'll need lots of steam, pressure, time, and patience.

Start with a good steam iron. I prefer an industrial iron because the steam blasts are much more powerful than the bursts of steam on regular steam irons. If you don't have one of these irons, place a piece of aluminum foil-covered cardboard under the garment to reflect the steam when pressing, and cover the garment with a damp press cloth.

Press all seams flat to blend the stitches in the fabric before pressing them open. Steam press open. Cover the seams with a clapper or fabric-covered brick. I actually spank the seams, as it causes the fibers to break down, making them more willing to accept a new position.

Do not move the pressed section until it is cool and dry. This is the biggest mistake most home sewers make.

Use a seam roll, point presser, or fabric-covered rolled magazine under the seam as you press. This prevents seam impressions on the outside of the garment.

The Elnapress® and other similar presses are like the pressing tables used in the fashion industry. They provide approximately 100 pounds of pressure on their beds. With practice, garments can be pressed with professional results. However, you must press as you sew and use pressing pads, to avoid pressing in unwanted wrinkles in shaped areas. You must also use strips of paper under seam allowances, to prevent seam impressions visible on the outside of the garment.

See also Irons.

Q

Q Recently, I used a pre-washed bedsheet to make a crib-sized comforter. I also used high-quality polyester batting and a cotton broadcloth backing. When I tried channel quilting on my machine, the results did not please me: skipped stitches followed by long, uneven stitch lengths interspersed with short, bunched-up stitches. I tried to adjust the tension, pressure, stitch length, and machine speed, with no luck. What can I do next time?

A According to Robbie Fanning, author of *The Complete Book of Machine Quilting*, these suggestions will help:

- Baste. Using large safety pins, baste the layers together. Space the pins close together in areas where they won't have to be removed while stitching.

- Use a walking foot (sometimes called a dual feeder, jumping foot, or even-feed). If you don't have a walking foot, try a roller foot or use a stabilizer like Stacy's Trace Erase™ between the fabric layers and the feed dogs.

- For easier handling, use the "stitch-and-rest" technique. When stitching long lengths that tend to creep, stop occasionally with the needle down, raise and lower the presser foot, and then continue stitching.

- Use a Schmetz jeans needle (705H-J) if it fits your machine. Sheets are more tightly woven than most fabrics, and the sharp point of this needle will penetrate densely woven fabrics. Try sizes 90/14 or 100/16. Be forewarned: this needle usually makes more noise than universal needles as it enters the fabric.

Use all-cotton thread or J&P Coats Dual Duty Plus® Extra Fine or all-polyester (100/3) thread. Many cotton-covered polyester core threads and 100% polyester threads are too thick for the needle and will fray and break.

R

Remodeling

Q I bought a camel hair coat at a thrift shop. The body of the coat is still fashionable, but the collar has long points. I'd like to update this coat with a fur collar. What do you suggest?

A To remodel the collar, you must first make an exact copy of the current collar. Thread trace the lengthwise grain at the center back of the collar. Mark the crosswise grain at right angles to it.

Smoothly pin pattern tracing cloth over the collar. Carefully trace the outer edges and neckline edges, and note matchpoints at the shoulder seams. Repeat this procedure for the undercollar. Reshape the collar points as desired.

Add 5/8" seam allowances to all edges, plus 1/4" to 3/8" to the outer edges to allow for the thickness of the fur.

Use this pattern to construct the new collar, using a lightweight lining fabric for the undercollar. Remove the old collar and set the new one.

See also Collars.

Repairs

Q I made a lovely silk charmeuse blouse with a tulle yoke and sleeves. I wore it to a party and came home with a cigarette burn at the top of one sleeve. Can I repair the hole without taking the blouse apart and replacing the sleeve?

A Repair the hole by hand as inconspicuously as possible. Then sprinkle and sew beads or sequins over the yoke and sleeves to create an interesting design and to conceal the mend.

See also Sequins and Beads.

Q Where can I find a list of fashion design schools?

Q The most recent issue of *Peterson's Annual Guide to Undergraduate Study* lists more than 125 schools with fashion design programs. Your local library should have this book in its reference section.

Schools

Q The side seams of my cotton-polyester blend skirts always pucker. I tried using a longer stitch length and holding the fabric firmly in front and behind the presser foot, but that doesn't seem to help. What more can I do?

A Puckered seams are particularly troublesome on lightweight, permanent press and tightly woven fabrics. Fabrics will often pucker when stitched in the direction of the least stretch, on the exact lengthwise grain.

These suggestions may help solve your annoying problem:

- Before stitching, check the tension to be sure it's balanced.
- Insert a new needle. Use the smallest size that will stitch a seam without skipping stitches; try 60(8), 70(10), or 75(11). A universal point needle is a good selection for most fabrics; however, for tightly woven fabrics, a sharp needle works better.
- Use the same type and weight of thread in the needle and bobbin. A lighter-than-normal weight of thread (100/3) will help reduce puckering.
- Set the stitch length to 12 to 15 stitches per inch (1.75mm to 2mm).
- Use a straight-stitch foot to hold the fabric firmly against the feed dogs. If you have only an all-purpose zigzag foot, move the

Seams

S ✄ ✄ ✄

Seams

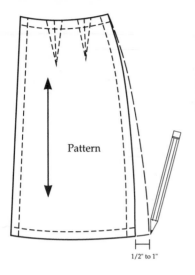

Pattern

1/2" to 1"

needle to the left- or right-hand position, depending on your brand of machine.

- Hold the fabric firmly in front and in back of the foot to prevent the machine from feeding the fabric too quickly. Stitch *slowly*.

- A stabilizer placed between the fabric and feed dogs will help reduce puckering on very lightweight fabrics.

- As a last resort, consider reshaping a straight-of-grain seam line to a slight bias grain, to eliminate dangers of puckers (see illustration).

See also Needle Hole.

Q What's the best way to finish seams on fabrics that fray? Seam sealants seems too stiff for some fabrics.

A Serging is the fastest and easiest way to control fraying. Other methods include:

- Enclosed seams, such as French, false-French, and standing fell seams are good choices for lightweight or sheer fabrics. (See my *Claire Shaeffer's Fabric Sewing Guide* for a complete discussion of seams and how to make them.)

- For medium- or heavyweight fabrics, finish the edges with a tricot binding, such as Seams Great® or Seam Saver™, a multi-step zigzag stitch, or a narrow strip of lightweight fusible interfacing applied to the wrong side of the seam allowance.

See also Fraying.

Q What's an effective seam finish for the curved armhole seam? Taping the edges hasn't worked for me.

A Several seam finishes can be used successfully on the armscye seam. To choose a seam finish, consider the quality and style of the garment, the amount of time you want to spend sewing, and the characteristics of the fabric—how much it frays, its crispness, and its weight or bulk.

Six finishes are listed below, in no particular order:

- Overcast the seam by hand.
- Using the machine, zigzag the edges together.
- Make a false or fake French seam by turning the raw edges in toward the seamline. Sew the folded edges together by hand or machine (see first illustration).
- Make a standing fell seam. Trim the sleeve seam allowance only to 1/8". Fold the raw edge of the garment seam allowance to meet the trimmed edge; then fold again, aligning the first fold with the stitching line. Hand or machine stitch the folded edge to the machine stitches (see second illustration).
- Encase the raw edges with Seams Great®, Seams Saver®, or cotton lace. Hand or machine stitch in place.
- Use a piece of bias-cut silk chiffon or China silk to bind the edges. It can be applied completely or partially by hand.

See also Sleeves.

Q How do you close a seam by hand when making a pillow or stuffed toy?

A There are several secrets to making a hand-sewn seam look like a machine-stitched one. Keeping the stitches short, use a ladder or a slipstitch approximately the same length as the machine stitches. Make the stitches so the threads which connect the two layers look exactly like a ladder, with no slanted steps. This makes the finished seam look like machine stitching.

Seams

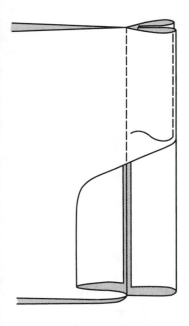

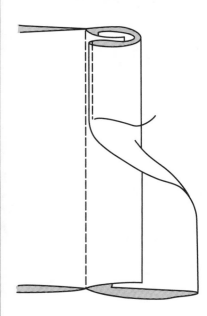

Seams

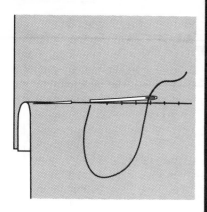

Here are four simple steps that will guide you in hand-sewing an invisible seam:

- Fold under one seam allowance and pin the opening closed.
- Fasten the thread and bring the needle from the inside of the pillow or toy out in the seamline.
- To make the first step in the ladder, insert the needle into the seamline of the other layer directly across from the thread exit hole.
- Take a short, 1/8" or less stitch, and go directly across to the other side, making another step in the ladder. Repeat until the opening is closed (see illustration).

Sequins and Beads

Q Can you recommend a fabric glue for applying pearls and beads to wedding gowns so the garments can be washed or drycleaned?

A Several drycleaners have told me that this is a common problem. They cannot tell before they begin cleaning if the beads will come off or stay on, and manufacturers don't tell which glues they used.

As a test, I glued bugle beads and sequin strips to a piece of silk crepe de chine, using several different glues. I then took the fabric to a quality drycleaner to be cleaned like a dress. The sample was cleaned with "perc," the fluid used by most drycleaners.

The results (which aren't scientific) were: Sobo and Aleene's Tacky glue held best. The other glues included Elmer's® Fabric Mender Cement, Unique Stitch, Velcro® Adhesive, Touch O Magic Fabric Cement, and Instant Vinyl. All are recommended for mending fabric.

You might want to perform a similar experiment with fabrics and beads you use most frequently.

If you sew for profit, inform your client of potential problems. Give her the option of paying more to have you sew the beads on by hand to guarantee their security. She could also choose to have you provide extra beads to be applied after cleaning. She may not want either choice, but by letting her make the decision, she assumes the responsibility.

See also Weddings.

Q When sewing children's skating costumes, we frequently use stretch material to make bands and belts. How do you sew sequins on stretch material so they are spaced evenly? Are there any helpful books on this subject?

A Bead Different, a resource specializing in theatrical trims and stretch fabrics for dancers and skaters, suggests making an appliqué first: sew the sequins to a lightweight backing fabric.

Pin the appliqué in place while the skater is wearing the costume. Ask the skater to remove the garment and secure the appliqué with hand or machine stitching.

If you're using individual sequins, use a water-soluble pen to mark their placements when the costume is on the skater.

An embroidery hoop is a great aid for holding the fabric in a stretched position while stitching. For machine stitching, use the hoop upside-down; that is, stretch the fabric over the outer ring and press the inner ring in place. Then tip the hoop under the presser foot (or remove the foot, if necessary, to slide the hoop in place).

Sequins and Beads

Sequins
and Beads

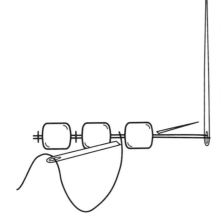

Bohana's Variations includes directions for making beaded appliqués, as well as a variety of appliqué designs to copy, available from Bead Different (see Bibliography).

Q Please give me details on how to apply sequins and beads. I have tried glue without success. I have also tried hand sewing, but they don't look neat. I made a flower appliqué and tried to outline it with beads, but it didn't work. Can you help?

A Depending on the look you want and the amount of time you have to invest, you have several choices for outlining designs. My work looks better and I can work faster if I use an embroidery hoop and a lamp with a magnifier.

- The easiest method utilizes a small decorative cord and doesn't even require beads. Pin the cord in place and secure it with small permanent stitches or use a machine zigzag (see first illustration).

- Another quick and easy method for outlining involves two threaded needles and small round or bugle beads. Anchor one of the threads and pull it to the right side of the garment. Thread the same needle with beads. Then use the other needle and thread to sew over the first, beaded thread. Use the second needle to move each bead into place, sewing between beads over the first thread and into the garment. Arrange the beads with or without spaces between them (see second illustration).

- If you like sequins, outline the beaded motif with an overlapping row of sequins. Working from right to left, bring the needle from the inside of the garment and into the back of the sequin. Hold it in place with your left thumb and take a very tiny stitch in the fabric to the left of the sequin. Repeat with each sequin (see third illustration).

As each new sequin is added, it should slightly overlap the one before it and cover the stitch that holds it in place.

- To sew sequins on individually, anchor a thread on the wrong side of the garment and bring it to the right side. Next slip a sequin, then a small bead, onto the needle and return the needle through the sequin into the fabric (see last illustration).

Sequins and Beads

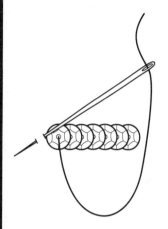

Q Do you have suggestions for sewing on sequinned fabrics? I want to make a special holiday dress.

A Sequinned fabrics have several characteristics which should be considered before you begin:

- They will dull scissors and needles.
- They have a nap.
- If the sequins are applied in a specific pattern, it should be matched.
- Sequin facings will irritate the skin. Substitute plain fabric facings instead.
- Sequins on the seam allowances of unlined garments will be especially uncomfortable. Rip the sequins from the seam allowances before you stitch the seams of the garment; then resew the sequins by hand at each seamline following the design on the fabric. If this is more time-consuming than the garment deserves, bind the raw edges with Seams Great® and wear a slip.
- You may decide to line the garment instead.

For more information, see my new book, *Claire Shaeffer's Fabric Sewing Guide* (see last page).

S

Shoulder
Pads

Q I don't like shoulder pads. Is it a crime not to use them sometimes?

A I think so. Shoulder pads are used in most ready-made garments. When you eliminate them, you immediately put a little tag on your garment that identifies it as "homemade."

More importantly, the addition of shoulder pads is a marvelous dieting aid for ample hips.

If you are lazy or don't like making them, purchase a bra with shoulder pads or add them to a bra you already have.

Q I look like a football player when I wear shoulder pads and would like to skip them altogether in my garments. How can I adjust patterns that call for shoulder pads?

A While shoulder pads may make you look like a football player, they also create an illusion of small hips and a slender body. Since they are in all of today's better ready-to-wear garments, those without shoulder pads tend to look home-made. Try thinner pads to find a look you like.

Cut out the front and back garment sections as indicated on the pattern. Do not cut the sleeves at this time.

Mark the stitching lines at the shoulders with thread tracing. Fold under the seam allowance of the front and pin it to the back. Stitch the underarm seams and try on the garment.

Insert thin shoulder pads, pin the garment closed, and look in the mirror. The wrinkles will make it look as though you have sloping shoulders. Beginning at the armscye and tapering to nothing at the neckline, pin out the excess fullness on the shoulder seams until the garment fits smoothly.

Remove the garment, repin the shoulder seam as it will be sewn, and try on the garment again. If you like what you see, stitch on the new seamline.

Remember to adjust the sleeve or facing pattern. To adjust the sleeve pattern, draw a line at right angles to the grainlines, midway between the shoulder point and first matchpoints. Cut on that line and lap the two sections the amount you've removed from the garment. For example, if you've pinned out 1/2" on the fold at the shoulder point, overlap 1/2". Redraw the cutting line and cut out the sleeves.

Shoulder Pads

Q When I use shoulder pads, a dimple often appears next to the neckline. At other times, a ridge appears at the edge of the pad. How can I prevent these?

A When the shoulder pad doesn't extend to the neckline seam, a dimple forms between the neckline and the edge of the pad. To avoid this, cut the top layer of the pad so its inside edge meets the edge of the seam allowances at the garment neckline.

To avoid a ridge at the edge of the shoulder pad, cut each of the shoulder pad's layers slightly smaller than the one above it. If you're making the pad from cotton batting or wadding, use your fingers to tear and feather the edges of the pad. Top the pad with a layer of muslin or hair canvas.

Sleeve Heads

Q I like the attractive lift that gives definition to the sleeve caps on expensive jackets. I can't seem to duplicate this look with Thermolam® sleeve heads or shoulder pads. Can you suggest something else?

A Designers sometimes create these crisp sleeve caps by underlining sleeves, as

S ✂ ✂ ✂

Sleeve Heads

well as using sleeve heads and shoulder pads. To recreate the look, consider the following:

- If you're making a wool jacket, the sleeve cap requires at least 2" of ease.
- If you underline the sleeves, use a lightweight, woven, sew-in interfacing. Pellon's Shapewell® and Stacy's Sta-Shape® provide crisper backings than organza or muslin.
- When using one of the crisper backings, cut it on the bias and slightly narrower than the garment, to fit smoothly inside the sleeve.
- For sleeve heads, use cotton wadding or batting. (Cotton wadding is available from tailoring supply houses; cotton batting is sold in quilting shops. If neither is available in your area, B. Black & Sons sells wadding and pre-made sleeve heads. A $25 minimum order is required. For information, send a pre-addressed stamped envelope to the address in the Resource List.)

To make sleeve heads:

- Cut a 2-1/2" x 8 1/2" piece of batting or wadding. Fold in half lengthwise (see first illustration). Baste layers together loosely with a large diagonal stitch.
- With the longer section toward the back of the sleeve, position the sleeve head with the folded edge overlapping the seamline 1/8" (see second illustration).
- Sew the sleeve heading in place with short running stitches.
- To avoid a ridge, feather or taper the cut edges of the heading with your fingers.
- Sew in the shoulder pads so they extend 5/8" into the sleeve cap.

See also Ease.

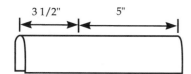

3 1/2"   5"

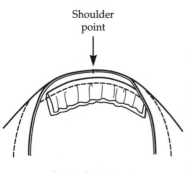

Shoulder point

Insert sleeve head into sleeve cap.

Sleeves

Q Is it possible to change a pattern with a dropped, extended shoulder to a regular set-in sleeve?

A The dropped, extended shoulder silhouette is designed with considerable fullness in the armscye and shoulder area. The sleeve cap is shaped very differently from that of a set-in sleeve. For these reasons, the conversion is a major pattern-drafting project I can't recommend.

Consider the use of shoulder pads to broaden or straighten your shoulder look in these garments.

Q Why are sleeves so difficult to stitch smoothly in linen-like and cotton/polyester blends?

A The ability to stitch sleeves easily and smoothly is determined by several factors: fiber content, fabric construction, sleeve design, and seam-allowance width.

Fibers such as wool, mohair, camel hair, and cashmere are easiest to sew smoothly into a sleeve, because they are easiest to shape with heat and moisture. Synthetic fibers (polyester and nylon) are the most difficult. Silk, cotton, linen, and blends fall somewhere in between. Similarly, firmly woven, plain-weave fabrics are more unwieldy than loosely woven, twill-weave, or knitted materials.

Sleeves designed with less ease are simpler to set-in smoothly. For most summer season fabrics, I prefer sleeves with about 1" ease in the cap. Using a see-through ruler or tape measure balanced on one edge, measure the armhole seamlines on the front and back bodies, notch to notch over the cap. Then measure the corresponding seamline on the sleeve cap (see first two illustrations).

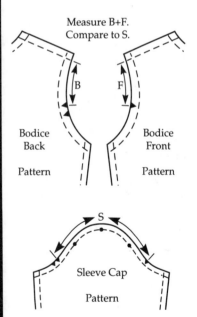

Measure B+F. Compare to S.

Bodice Back Pattern

Bodice Front Pattern

Sleeve Cap Pattern

Sleeves

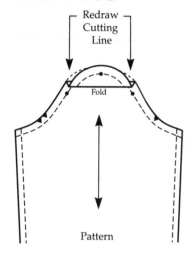

Redraw Cutting Line

Fold

Pattern

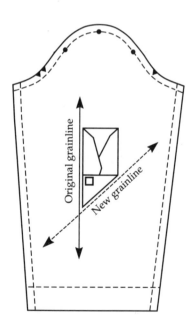

Original grainline

New grainline

The difference between the two measurements is the amount of sleeve cap ease. In this case, if the ease is more than 1", make the pattern correction before cutting out the fabric.

Fold a horizontal tuck through the top of the sleeve cap. A tiny 1/8" tuck will remove almost 1/2" of ease. Redraw the cutting lines without reducing the cap width (see third illustration).

An alternate solution is to cut the sleeves on the bias. This works best for firmly woven, mediumweight fabric, like bridal satin or peau de soie. A few lighter weight fabric sleeves will stretch or bag out-of-shape if cut on the bias.

To mark the grainline for the bias-cut sleeve, fold an envelope so that one short end matches one long side. Align the side of the envelope with the grainline; draw the new grainline at the folded edge (see fourth illustration).

Narrower seam allowances are also easier to stitch than wider ones. Trim the armscye seam allowances on the garment and sleeve to 1/2" before setting in the sleeve.

Use two rows of ease-basting: one just inside the seamline and the other midway between the seamline and the raw edge. And if needle holes won't mar the fabric, place an additional row 3/4" from the edge.

This is my favorite ease-basting method, although there are many others. Fill the bobbin with polyester topstitching thread; loosen the upper tension. With a regular stitch length, sew with the sleeve right side up. Lengthen the stitch as necessary for heavier fabrics, but if the stitch is too long for the fabric weight, it will pleat instead of ease the cap.

To avoid a dimple from forming at the notch, I begin and end the ease-basting 1/2" beyond the notches. Then I adjust the ease, pulling the bobbin threads to ease the sleeve cap and keeping the first and last 1/2" flat. Pull both bobbin threads together, to reduce strain, prevent broken threads, and adjust the ease smoothly. Use a pin at each end; secure the threads at one end by wrapping them around the pin in a figure eight (see fifth illustration).

With the fabric wrong side up, insert a pressing mitt into the sleeve cap. Steam press the ease-basting rows without allowing the iron point to extend more than 1/2" into the sleeve cap (see sixth illustration).

Right sides together, baste and stitch the sleeve into the armhole. To eliminate any additional dimples, use sleeve heads of bias-cut self-fabric, interfacing, Seams Great® or SeamSaver®. See Shoulder Pads for an easy sleeve head.

Q I've made a number of blouses that seem to have too much fabric at the top of the sleeve. The designs are ordinary sleeves, not excessively gathered or puffed. Should I be checking the amount of ease in the sleeves on every blouse pattern I buy? I thought the designers knew what they were doing. Also, is it too late to correct what I've done?

A Yes, you should automatically check sleeve ease for every pattern (see previous question), just as you check other measurements. You should not have more than 1-1/2" ease on blouse patterns; on lightweight fabric, I prefer about 1" ease. If you need to remove some ease, see the previous question.

No, it's not too late to correct what you've done. You have four choices:

- Add a sleeve head (see Sleeve Heads and Ease).

Sleeves

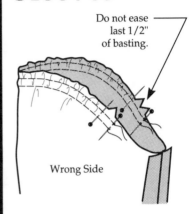

Do not ease last 1/2" of basting.

Wrong Side

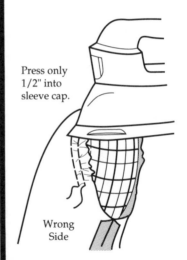

Press only 1/2" into sleeve cap.

Wrong Side

Sleeves

- Take out the stitching and drop the notches on the sleeve 1/4" below those on the garment. That way, you can add 1/2" more ease toward the underarm. This is my first choice, because it leaves the cap in.
- Take out the stitching between the notches and over the cap. Trim the sleeve cap 1/8" at the shoulder point, tapering to nothing at the first matchpoint. Trimming 1/8" here will remove 3/8" ease.
- Take out the stitching between the notches and over the cap. Pin the sleeve cap into the armscye so that the sleeve has a 3/4" seam allowance, tapering the seam allowance to 5/8" at the matchpoints. The seam allowance on the garment doesn't change.

I also like to handbaste the sleeve into the garment, because I can control the ease better.

See also Ease.

Q I do alterations on menswear in a department store and have noticed that the caps on ready-to-wear jacket sleeves are smooth at the front and back. When I sew with commercial patterns, I can't get the sleeves smooth because there's too much ease in the back. Do ready-to-wear jackets have all the ease removed?

A No, manufacturers do not remove the ease in the sleeve cap. In fact, ready-to-wear jackets frequently have more ease than commercial patterns. I sometimes add ease to the sleeve cap so the sleeve will hang more attractively. I rarely remove it, except to correct the fit for a particular figure type.

These suggestions should help you get a smooth set:

- Check the ease in the sleeve (see previous question). Most fabrics can be eased at least 1". Loosely woven materials and woolens can be eased as much as 3" or 4".

- Make two rows of ease stitching on the sleeve cap, placing one almost, but not quite, on the seamline and the other 3/8" from the raw edge. If the fabric will not be marred by needle holes, place a third row 3/4" from the edge. Pull up the ease stitching so the cap will fit the armhole. I mark a piece of twill tape with the same markings (dots or notches) as are on the armscye and use it as a guide.

- On the sleeve back, distribute the ease evenly between the notches and shoulder point to fit the rounded back shoulder. On the front, concentrate more ease in the upper half of the sleeve to fit the body's protruding shoulder bone.

If the pattern indicates no ease is allowed at the top of the sleeve, disregard this instruction. Without ease at the top of the cap, there will be no room for the seam allowances and sleeve head. The cap will look flat and there will be too much ease to distribute in the rest of the sleeve. Allow just a tiny bit (1/8" to 1/4") at the top.

- With the right side out, place the cap over the end of the sleeve board or a pressing pad. Mold the cap into shape, using steam and shrinking out the fullness in the seam allowance only. Do not allow the point of the iron to extend into the sleeve cap more than 1/4". Use a Steamstress® or shot-of-steam iron to eliminate the need for a press cloth.

- Baste and stitch the sleeves into the garment. Insert shoulder pads and sleeve heads—two essential ingredients for smooth caps in tailored garments and in some current blouse styles.

See also Seams.

Sleeves

Sleeves

Q Some of my blouse patterns have gathers at the sleeve cap, but I'd like to remove them so the cap can be eased in smoothly. Have you ever done this?

A In addition to the pattern you've selected, choose another pattern with the desired sleeve style. The two armscyes must be compatible. You can't take a sleeve from a pattern with a cropped shoulder and set it into a design with a regular armscye. Avoid interchanging blouse and jacket sleeves and try to use patterns made by the same pattern company.

On both patterns, fold and pin out any shoulder fullness (darts, pleats, tucks, or gathers). Lay the original bodice front over the new pattern, matching center fronts and shoulder points. Trace the cutting and seam lines from the new pattern to the original along the shoulder seam and around the armscye. Blend the underarm seam together. Mark all matchpoints. Repeat on the pattern back.

Cut out the garment using the altered original pattern, with a new armscye shaping and a new sleeve pattern.

Q I have trouble measuring sleeve and arm lengths for garments with dropped shoulder lines, kimono, raglan, or dolman sleeves. Can you help?

A On some patterns, there is no way to accurately measure the sleeve length. However, the problem can be solved if you use your previous experiences and knowledge as a guide.

Ask a friend to measure your arm from the shoulder point to just below the prominent bone on the little finger side of your wrist. Your arm should hang relaxed, close to your side (see first illustration). Many home sewers

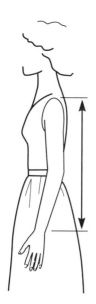

have mistakenly held the arm bent at a right angle, resulting in a measurement much too long.

Select a classic, set-in sleeve pattern with a dart and natural armscye. Beginning at the shoulder point, measure the sleeve length parallel to the grainline (see second illustration).

Compare the two measurements. The sleeve measurement is frequently 1/2" to 3/4" longer than the body measurement, depending on how much the designer added for the sleeve cap. If it differs, determine how much you need to lengthen or shorten the pattern. Theoretically, this is the amount you will use to adjust sleeves on all patterns; unfortunately, pattern companies don't agree on the average arm length.

If you want a perfect fit, make the basic garment in muslin.

Q When I turn spaghetti straps right side out, my stitches break. How can I make tiny, firm strips?

A The secret to eliminating broken stitches is to stretch the bias strip as much as possible when stitching.

The finished size of spaghetti straps or self-filled bias tubing is determined by the type of fabric used. Tubings made from soft, lightweight, silky materials will be skinnier than those made from fabrics that are stiff, mediumweight, or rough in texture.

The following will help you make the smallest possible tubings from any fabric:

- Cut a 1-1/2"-wide strip on the true bias. It should be cut the desired length without any pieced seams. If the tubing will be used for button loops or other short trim-

Sleeves

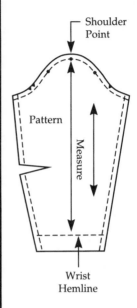

Shoulder Point

Pattern

Measure

Wrist Hemline

Spaghetti Straps

Spaghetti Straps

Trim ——

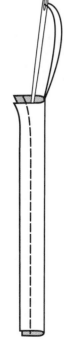

mings, stitch short strips. They're easier to handle than one long strip.

- Shorten the stitch length to 1 mm or 1.5 mm (20 to 25 inches per inch).
- Fold the strip in half lengthwise, with right sides together.
- Stitch a small "funnel" at the beginning of the strip and continue stitching close to the fold, stretching the strip as much as possible. The strip will narrow when stretched, making the stitched line on lightweight blouse fabrics only 1/16" from the fold.
- Trim the seam allowances so the stitched line is in the center of the strip (see first illustration). Trim even closer next to the funnel.
- Using a small tapestry needle and a doubled short length of buttonhole twist, fasten the thread securely into the fold at the top of the funnel (see second illustration). Thread the needle into the tubing and pull the strip right side out. To start the turn easily, moisten your thumb and forefinger with a little saliva.
- For very tiny smooth tubings, wet the entire strip, squeeze dry in a towel, and pin in a stretched position to your ironing board or pressing ham. Be sure the seamline is straight. Water spotting is not a problem, since you wet the entire strip.

Stitch Length

Q I have a European machine with different numbers than my old Singer. When I read instructions for stitches per inch, what setting should I use?

A European machines use metrics. Usually 2-2.5 on your stitch length dial or lever corresponds to 10-12 stitches per inch. A 4 setting is for basting. Every machine differs. Make a straight stitch sample on 1"-square gingham or gridded pattern tracing cloth. Label the setting you used and count the number of stitches per inch. Label that, too. Then pin the sample in the margin of this book.

T

T-shirts

Q When I buy T-shirts with a knitted band at the waistline, they are too long. I have tried shortening them by removing the band, cutting off the desired amount, and then resewing the band to the shirt. Alas—it is always too short. What am I doing wrong?

A Maybe you have forgotten to include the seam allowance or maybe you have removed all the ease. T-shirts with bands at the waist usually have 1/2" to 1" vertical ease above the band.

To avoid too-short T-shirts, put on the garment. Pin a horizontal tuck on the top to make it the desired length. Remove the top and measure the entire tuck width.

Remove the band and shorten the top an amount equal to the tuck width.

Thread

Q Cone thread has strange sizes on it—100/2, 50/2, and 40/3. What do these numbers mean?

A The first number is the thread size; the higher the number, the finer the thread. The second number is the number of plies or strands twisted together to make the thread.

Generally, three-ply thread is used for garment construction and two-ply thread, for finishing edges and for machine embroidery.

Q I have a lot of old cotton thread. Can it still be used?

A Cotton thread has less strength and stretch than synthetic threads. It may be used for hand and machine stitching on woven, natural fiber fabrics, but it isn't suitable for knits or synthetic fabrics. If it isn't mercerized, it will shrink when the garment is washed. It may not be colorfast and may bleed onto the background if you use it for basting.

Because your thread is old, it has probably dried out and become brittle. But cotton is stronger when wet, so it may still be usable. Wet the thread, spool and all. When dry, it'll be as strong as new thread.

Q Which is better for machine stitching, cotton-covered polyester or long-staple polyester thread? How will these threads affect my machine?

A Cotton-covered polyester and long-staple polyester are both good-quality threads. Both are excellent for machine work on most fabrics, particularly on synthetics and blends. For most silk fabrics, I still prefer mercerized cotton thread, so the thread will break before the fabric tears.

Although polyester, which is an oil by-product and a form of plastic, is abrasive, the amount of machine damage it causes is insignificant compared to the damage that can be caused by the lint from fabrics. The secret is to keep your machine clean and lint free. Fortunately, good-quality threads have little lint.

Use a clean, dry dishwasher liquid bottle to blow out the lint when you finish sewing each day. If you're embroidering, appliquéing, or sewing on synthetic fabrics or polyester fleece, lint will accumulate very quickly, and you should clean your machine several times during the day. If most of your sewing is straight stitching, use a straight-stitch needle plate to reduce the accumulation of lint between the feed dogs.

A clean machine will reward you with fewer skipped stitches and puckered seams.

T

Travel

Q I plan to visit New York City this year and would like to see some fashion-related sights. Do you have any suggestions?

A There are so many things to see in New York, you'll have trouble deciding what to see first. Two areas are of major interest to home sewers: the areas around FIT and around the Metropolitan.

The museum at the Fashion Institute of Technology (FIT) is at 227 West 27th St., at the corner of Seventh Ave. Check for their current exhibit. Museum hours are Tuesday, 10-9; Wednesday through Saturday, 10-5.

There are many fabric, notions, and clothing outlets within walking distance of FIT.

The Costume Institute, downstairs at the Metropolitan Museum of Art, usually has wonderful exhibits. The museum is located on Fifth Avenue at 82nd St. Call for current hours; the museum, like many, is closed on Mondays. Please note: no sketching is allowed in the Costume Institute exhibits.

The area near the Met is full of interesting places: the Guggenheim, the Cooper-Hewitt (the design museum of the Smithsonian), the Museum of Modern Art, the Museum of Contemporary Crafts, Julie's Artisan Crafts, Tiny Buttons (a shop full of buttons), and more.

In addition, not far from the Met are such high-fashion stores as Bloomingdale's at Lexington and 59th, Bergdorf Goodman at 754 Fifth Ave. at 58th St., and Saks Fifth Avenue at the corner of Fifth Ave. and 50th St.

Although cabs are relatively inexpensive in New York, you can take the bus quite easily to all of the above. Ask what the current fare is; you will need exact change.

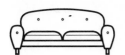 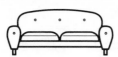 

U

Q One of my clients wants an expensive Ultrasuede® suit shortened. The hem is so well-glued that I can't open it up. When I apply steam and heat, the fabric stretches. What can I do?

A To prevent stretching, do not try to unfuse the hem before shortening the garment. Mark the new hemline with chalk, soap, or an air-soluble pen. Then machine stitch through all layers 1/16" above the marked line. Trim on the marked line and machine stitch again 1/2" from the edge (see first illustration).

If you want to shorten the hem several inches or more than the width of the existing hem allowance, consider this method:

- Mark the new hemline.
- Mark again 1/4" below the hemline. Then trim on the second line.
- From the hem you've just cut off, cut a 1"-wide facing strip.
- Wrong sides together, "baste" the facing strip to the garment with washable glue stick.
- Machine stitch a fat 1/4" from the raw edges.
- Trim just below the stitched line and stitch again 1/2" from the edge (see second illustration).

Q I sent my Ultrasuede® coat to the drycleaners and it came back limp. Should I wash my Ultrasuede® garments instead of having them drycleaned?

A The coat can be washed if it's a purchased garment with a washable care label or if it's a hand-sewn garment with preshrunk, washable linings and interfacings. However, each time you wash it, the fabric will become a bit softer.

Ultrasuede

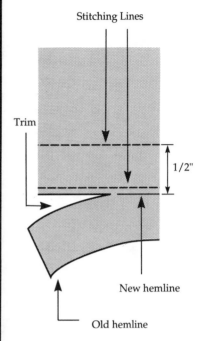

Stitching Lines

Trim

1/2"

New hemline

Old hemline

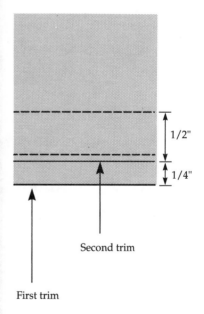

1/2"

1/4"

Second trim

First trim

U

Ultrasuede

Q I'd like to make a garment from Glore-Valcana suede. Is there anything special I need to know to sew on it?

A Glore-Valcana is a synthetic suede similar to Ultrasuede® and Lamous. Here are some hints for sewing with synthetic suedes:

- Pretest the pattern, correct the fit, and wash the fabric before cutting.
- Use a "with nap" layout.
- To prevent skipped stitches, use a new Schmetz universal or Singer Yellow-band needle (size 11 or 14) and a needle lubricant.
- To prevent the underlayer from creeping, use an even-feed or walking foot, or secure the layers with water-soluble basting tape or glue stick.
- To avoid splitting the fabric, lengthen the stitch to 8 to 10 stitches per inch. Also, try to avoid ripping, which may leave permanent needle holes and weaken the fabric.
- To avoid puckered seams, hold the fabric firmly in front of and behind the presser foot when stitching.
- When hand sewing, use a thimble and a leather needle.
- Press from the wrong side or use a press cloth.
- Since seams won't stay open after pressing, topstitch or use a fusing agent to hold the seam allowances in place.

For additional information, see my new book, *Claire Shaeffer's Fabric Sewing Guide.*

See also Appliqués, Interfacings.

Q My rib cage is large and extends almost to my waistline. If I make a 1-1/4"-wide waistband that fits at my waistline, it is too tight at the top of the band. But if I make it large enough to fit the top, it's too large at the waist. What can I do?

A This Yves Saint Laurent technique will solve your problem.

- Cut the waistband on the crossgrain, so that it is twice the desired width plus 2" and the desired length plus 6".

- Fold the band in half lengthwise, wrong sides together. With a steam iron and damp press cloth, shape the band so the folded edge is longer than the cut edges. The amount of shaping will depend on your figure.

- Measure and mark the finished width (1-1/4") plus one seam allowance (5/8") from the foldline. Trim both layers of the band on the marked line.

- Mark the finished length of the band at the cut edges. Be certain to include the underlap and/or overlap and seam allowances at each end.

- Cut or shape the interfacings to fit the band.

- Now when you set the band to the pants, the folded edge will flare out and fit your rib cage attractively.

Waistbands

Waistbands

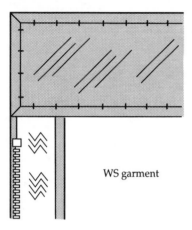

WS garment

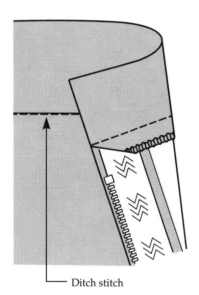

Ditch stitch

Q I don't like the bulk at the ends of waistbands on pants or skirts. I think it makes my garments look unprofessional. Do you have a better way to handle this area?

A There are several solutions to eliminating bulk. For each method, be certain to grade the seam allowances so that the one toward the outside of the garment is the longest.

- The first method works well on most fabrics. Place the garment on a firm surface, but not on an ironing board, as it has too much padding and is too resilient. If necessary, place the garment on a wooden floor covered with a clean cloth. Use a Steamstress® or an iron with a damp pressing cloth to fill each end of the waistband with steam. Then, using a clapper, pound the steam out to flatten the waistband ends.

- If the garment fabric is particularly bulky, cut the waistband facing (the inside of the band) from lining fabric or use grosgrain ribbon. This is a favorite designer trick and the facing is frequently applied to the inside of the band by hand (see first illustration).

- Unless you prefer a clean-finished band with all the seam allowances enclosed within the finished band, use the stitch-in-the-ditch method to apply the waistband. It creates less bulk at the top of the placket (see second illustration).

Weddings

Q I'm making a bridal gown with taffeta ruffles that border the skirt. The ruffles are gathered through the center. I find it easier to stitch these to the skirt if I use three gathering rows instead of one. The trouble is that this method leaves permanent needle holes in the fabric when I remove the gathering threads. What do you suggest?

A Taffeta is easily marred by machine stitching. It may not be possible to avoid permanent holes, but you can minimize them.

- Select a very small needle—size 60/8—and a good-quality polyester thread. Lengthen the stitch to eight stitches per inch.
- Use two, instead of three, rows of gathering stitches, placed 1/8" apart. Gather the ruffles, pin them to the skirt, and topstitch between the gathered rows. Generally, the fullness of the ruffles will hide the gathering threads.

If you're not happy with the look, consider covering the gathering threads with soutache braid, pearl cotton, lace, or a small round cord.

See also Presser Feet.

Q My daughter is getting married in June. What do we do with the train of her dress at the reception?

A Marla Hill, a specialist in bridal alterations, came to the rescue with this technique for making a bustle back. She guarantees that the bride can dance all night without embarassing the dressmaker.

- While the bride-to-be has the dress on, find the center back seam. Experiment with picking up the center back seam midway between the waist and the bottom of the train. Pin it to the waistline seam or the bottom of the zipper, so that the end

W

Weddings

of the train grazes the floor. This pick-up point will vary with the garment design and the length of the train. Move it up or down as needed.

- Unpin the bustle and mark the pick-up point with one pin on the center back seam. Help the bride remove the dress.
- Wrong side up, begin stitching 2" above the pin, stitch toward the pin, and stop 1/8" before reaching it. With the needle down, turn the garment around and stitch the 2" again.
- Repeat on the seamline below the pick-up point.
- Break the stitches on the original seamline at the pin, remove the pin, and press the seam open.
- Use a 2" piece of 1" twill tape to reinforce the seam. Fold it in half crosswise and place the folded edge on top of the seam allowances at the bottom of the little hole. Sew the tape securely to the seam allowances.
- Sew a hook to the tape and seam allowances, so the end of the hook can be pushed through the little hole.
- Use a crochet hook to make a thread eye at the waistline seam.

Now the bride can lift at the fold, hook it to the waistline, and dance all night.

Each dress will differ slightly, so you may need to modify these instructions. If the skirt has more than one layer, all layers will be held up, but only the bottom one should be reinforced. If the dress has a very short train, place the thread eye at the bottom of the zipper instead of at the waistline seam.

Another method I like was inspired by a Schiaparelli evening coat. It had decorative self-filled tubing at the waist in the shape of a flower. One of the flower petals formed a

button loop which could be looped over a ball button on the skirt.

If either of these methods does not appeal, make a wrist loop from the dress fabric and sew it to the end of the train.

Q What is the easiest way to make a narrow hem on the ruffles of a silk organza wedding gown?

A This hemming technique from Francis Cowan at Sew Magnifique in Atlanta is called a fine finish. She used it on her daughter's bridal gown and it was gorgeous.

- Allowing a 5/8" hem allowance, stitch on the hemline.
- Fold under the hem allowance along the stitching line. If your machine has a foot designed to avoid feed dog tracks, be certain to use it.
- With the right side up, center the fold under the needle and zigzag over the edge, so that the needle swings off the fabric on the right side.
- Using 5" trimmers and the "palms-up" technique, trim the excess hem allowance: hold the scissors in your right hand with your thumb in the handle of the large blade. Proceed with both palms up. Hold the garment in your left hand with the wrong side up and the raw edge of the hem toward your body. Position the large blade of the scissors under the hem allowance; trim close to the zigzag stitching.

This finish is particularly attractive and can be used on a variety of fabrics by varying the stitch width and length, but if you don't trim closely enough, it may ravel slightly after washing.

Z

Zippers

Q Whatever happened to self-basting zippers? I am a dressmaker and these zippers were so easy to press-baste into a garment for the customer's fitting, but I haven't seen them recently.

A Self-basting zippers were made by Wrights. When the manufacturing costs escalated, the zippers were discontinued. If you like the press-basting technique, you can make your own self-basting zippers.

Cut strips of Wonder-Under™, Fine Fuse™, or Transfuse® II. Place the strips on the right side of the zipper tape, and fuse the strips in place. Press-baste the zipper into the garment.

Q I make ladies' garment bags and need long, heavy-duty zippers. Where can I buy them?

A Many upholstery shops sell heavy-duty zippers by the inch. Also try the catalog from Home-Sew (see Resource List).

To sew across these heavy zippers easily at the top and bottom, make fabric stops.

Cut the stop 3" long and the width of the closed zipper and tape. Fold the fabric in half crosswise, wrong sides together. Right sides up, place the stop over the bottom (or top of the zipper), so the edges of the fabric match the edges of the zipper tape. Machine stitch the stop to the zipper tape. Trim away the zipper teeth under the stop .

Resource List

Note: Many of these are small businesses. As a matter of courtesy, please enclose a business-sized self-addressed stamped envelope when inquiring. For more complete listings than I have room, consult **The Sew-by-Mail Directory** *by Leslie Wood ($3.95 from Update Newsletters, 2269 Chestnut, Ste 269, San Francisco, CA 94123) and* **Designer Source Listing, Volume III** *by Maryanne Burgess ($10.45 from Carikean Publishing, PO Box 1171, Chicago, IL 60611).*

Aardvark
PO Box 2449
Livermore, CA 94550
$1 catalog

American Home Sewing Assoc.
1375 Broadway
New York, NY 10018

American Sewing Guild
PO Box 50936
Indianapolis, IN 46250

Bead Different
7 W. Quincy
Westmont, IL 60557

Britex-by-Mail
146 Geary St.
San Francisco, CA 94108
$3 swatches

Burda Patterns, Inc.
PO Box 2517
Smyrna, GA 30081

Classic Cloth
2508 McMullen Booth Rd.
Clearwater, FL 34621

Clothing Design Concepts
Box 1188
Manhattan, KS 66502

Clotilde
PO Box 22312
Ft. Lauderdale, FL 33335

Coats & Clark
Consumer Service Dept.
PO Box 1010
Toccoa, GA 30577

Daisy Kingdom
134 N.W. 8th
Portland, OR 97209

Donner Designs, Inc.
Box 7217
Reno, NV 89510

The Fabric Carr
170 State St.
Los Altos, CA 94022

Fairchild Publications
see F.I.T.

Fashion Touches
Box 804
Bridgeport, CT 06601

Bette Feinstein
Hard-to-Find Needlework Books
96 Roundwood Rd
Newton, MA 02164

F.I.T. Bookstore
227 W. 27th St
New York, NY 10001

Fit for You
781 Golden Prados Dr.
Diamond Bar, CA 91765

Folkwear
This company is recently out of business. Check the ads in "Sew News" for other companies still selling their patterns.

G Street Fabrics
11854 Rockville Pike
Rockville, MD 20852

Ghee's
106 E. Kings Hwy, Ste 205
Shreveport, LA 71104
$1 catalog

Green Pepper, Inc.
941 Olive St.
Eugene, OR 97401
$2 catalog

Jean Hardy Pattern Co.
2151 La Cuesta Dr.
Santa Ana, CA 92705
$1 catalog

Home-Sew
Bethlehem, PA 18018
$.50 catalog

Iowa Pigskin Sales Co.
Box 115
Clive, IO 50053

Joanne's Creations
2026 E. Cairo Dr.
Tempe, AZ 85282
$1 catalog

Kieffer's
1625 Hennepin Ave.
Minneapolis, MN 55403

Kwik-Sew Pattern Co.
3000 Washington Ave North
Minneapolis, MN 55411

Lacis
2982 Adeline St
Berkeley, CA 94703

Leonora's Patterns
c/o Tacony Corporation
1760 Gilsinn Lane
Fenton, MO 63026

Nancy's Notions
PO Box 683
Beaver Dam, WI 53916
catalog free, $1 swatches

Newark Dressmaker Supply
PO Box 2448
Lehigh Valley, PA 18001

Oregon Tailor Supply Co.
2123A S.E. Division St.
Portland, OR

Past Patterns
PO Box 7587
Grand Rapids, MI 49510
$5 catalog or free information

Pauloa Patterns
Box 11254
Honolulu, HI 96828
$1 catalog

The Perfect Notion
566 Hoyt St.
Darien, CT 06820
$1 catalog

Redlands Sewing Center
422 E. State St.
Redlands, CA 92373

SewCraft
Box 1869
Warsaw, IN 46580
$2 sample

Sew/Fit Co.
PO Box 565
LaGrange, IL 60525

Sewing Emporium
1087 Third Ave.
Chula Vista, CA 92010
$2 catalog

Sew Magnifique
3220 Paces Ferry Pl NW
Atlanta, GA 30305
$1 swatches

Jane Shaner
311 Valley Brook Rd.
McMurray, PA 15317

Solar-Kist Corp.
PO Box 273
LaGrange, IL 60525

Stretch & Sew Patterns
PO Box 185
Eugene, OR 97440

Tailor-Craft
4003 W. Armour St.
Seattle, WA 98119

Tandy Leather Co.
Box 2934

Fort Worth, TX 76113

Treadleart
25834-I Narbonne Ave.
Lomita, CA 90717
$1.50 catalog

Wooden Porch Books
Rt. 1 Box 262
Middlebourne, WV 26149
$3/3 catalogs

The World in Stitches
82 South St.
Milford, NH 03055

Publications:

Bias Line
Costume Tech
115 S. Manhattan
Tampa, FL 33609
$2 sample issue

Creative Needle
PO Box 99
Lookout Mtn., GA 37350
$5.50 sample issue

Homesewing Trade News
PO Box 286
Rockville Centre, NY 11571

Needlecraft for Today
PO Box 2011
Harlan, IO 51537

Sew Business
15400 Knoll Trail Dr
Dallas, TX 75248
$15/year

Sew It Seams
PO Box 2698
Kirkland, WA 98083
$4 sample

Sew News
Box 1790
Peoria, IL 61656

Sewing Update Newsletter
Serging Update Newsletter
2269 Chestnut Ste 269
San Francisco, CA 94123
$3.50 sample

Threads
63 S. Main St.
Newton, CT 06470

Bibliography

Note: Your public librarian can help you find these books through Interlibrary Loan.

Anderson, Barbara and Cletus, *Costume Design*, Holt, Rinehart, & Winston, New York, 1984, $28.95.

Armstrong, Helen Joseph, *Patternmaking for Fashion Design*, c/o F.I.T. Bookstore, $33.25.

Bame, Louise, *Pants Fit for Your Figure*, Vista Publications (830 26th St, Santa Monica, CA 94043), $11.50.

Bohana's Variations, Bead Different (7 West Quincy, Westmont, IL 60557).

Brinkley, Jeanne and Aletti, Ann, *Altering Ready-to-Wear Fashions*, Charles A. Bennett Publishing Co (809 Detweiller Dr., Peoria, IL 61615), 1976, $20.48.

Cabrera and Meyers, *Classic Tailoring Techniques: A Construction Guide for Men's Wear*, Fairchild Publications, Inc., New York, 1983, $20.

Coffin, David, *The Custom Shirt Book*, c/o "Threads" Magazine, Box 355, Newtown, CT 06470.

Dodson, Jackie and Ahles, Carol, *Know Your Elna*, Chilton Book Co., 1988, $12.95 (available from PO Box 2634, Menlo Park, CA 94026 after 12/15/88, along with *Know Your* books for Bernina, New Home, Pfaff, Viking, and a generic *Know Your Sewing Machine*--add $2 postage).

Fanning, Robbie and Tony, *The Complete Book of Machine Quilting*, Chilton Book Co., 1978, $16.95 postpaid from PO Box 2634, Menlo Park, CA 94026.

Gaino-Roberts, Susan, *The Thread-Line*, Jefferson County Adult Education (10801 W. 44th St., Wheatridge, CO 80033).

Gioello, Debbie and Berke, Beverly, *Figure Types and Size Ranges*, Fairchild Publications, New York, 1979, $20.

Handford, Jack, *Professional Patternmaking for Designers: Women's Wear, Men's Casual Wear*, Plycon Press (Box 220, Redondo Beach, CA 90277), 1984, $18.95.

Holkeboer, Kathering Strand, *Patterns for Theatrical Costumes*, Prentice-Hall, Inc., Englewood Cliffs, NJ 07632, 1984, $14.95.

Hollen, Norma, Patternmaking by the Flat-Pattern Method, Macmillan, 1987.

Ingham, Rosemary and Covey, Elizabeth, *The Costume Designer's Handbook*, Prentice-Hall, Inc., Englewood Cliffs, NJ, 1983, $24.95.

Ingham, Rosemary and Covey, Elizabeth, *The Costumer's Handbook*, Prentice-Hall, Inc., Englewood Cliffs, NJ 07632, 1979, $12.95.

Johnson, Beryl, *Advanced Embroidery Techniques*, David and Charles, c/o The World in Stitches (82 South St., Milford, NH 03055), 1983, $30.95.

Johnson, Mary, *Mary Johnson's Guide to Altering and Restyling Ready-Made Clothes*, E.P. Dutton & Co., New York, out of print.

Kawashima, Masaaki, *Fundamentals of Men's Fashion Design: A Guide to Tailored Clothes*, Fairchild Publications, New York, 1976, $18.50.

Kawashima, Masaaki, *Men's Outerwear Design*, Fairchild Publications, New York, 1976, $18.50.

Know Your Sewing Machine series of books—see Dodson.

Kopp, Rolfo, Zelin, & Gross, *Designing Apparel Through the Flat Pattern*, Fairchild Publications, New York, 1972, $24.95.

Ladbury, Ann, *The Dressmaker's Dictionary*, Arco Publishers, New York, out of print.

The Ladies' Guide to Needle Work, R.L. Shep (Box 668, Mendocino, CA 95460), 1986, $9.95.

Leiter, James C., Jr., and Stanley, Joan, *Discover Dressmaking as a Professional Career*, out of print.

Leopold, Allison Kyle and Cloutier, Anne Marie, *Short Chic*, Bantam Books, Inc., New York, 1987, $9.95.

MacIntosh, Eileen, *Sewing and Collecting Vintage Fashions*, Chilton Book Co., 1988, $14.95 postpaid from PO Box 2634, Menlo Park, CA 94026.

Master Designer, *Modern Garment Design and Grading Clothing for Men and Boys*, Master Designer (343 S. Dearborn St., Chicago, IL 60604), $20.

Peterson's Annual Guide to Undergraduate Study, see your local library.

Price, Jeanne and Zamkoff, Bernard, *Grading Techniques for Modern Designing*, Fairchild Publications, New York, 1973, $17.50.

Rivers, Belle, *Yes, You Can Alter Ready-to-Wear*, Dritz Corporation (PO Box 5028, Spartanburg, SC 29304), 50 cents.

Roberts, Edmund B., and Onishenko, Gary, *Fundamentals of Men's Fashion Design: A Guide to Casual Clothes*, Fairchild Publications, New York, 1985, $18.50.

Roehr, Mary A., *Altering Men's Ready-to-Wear*, (PO Box 1967, Memphis, TN 38101), 1987, $12.95.

Roehr, Mary A., *Altering Women's Ready-to-Wear*, address above, 1987, $17.95.

Roehr, Mary A., *Sewing as a Home Business*, address above.

Rohr, M., *Grading Women's and Misses Garment Design*, c/o FIT Bookstore.

Scheier, M., *ABC's of Grading*, c/o F.I.T. Bookstore, $10.95.

"Sewing for Profit," Bulletin #208, Cooperative Extension Service, Ohio State University, Columbus, OH 43210.

Shaeffer, Claire--see last page for full list of books.

Vogue Sewing Book, Harper & Row, New York, 1982, $24.95.

Zamkoff, Barnard and Price, Jeanne, *Basic Pattern Skills for Fashion Design*, Fairchild Publications, New York, 1987, $17.50.

The Last Page

Share your love of sewing with a friend: order him or her another copy of this book from:

Sewing S.O.S.
PO Box 2634-B
Menlo Park, CA 94026
$12 postpaid ($12.65, California residents)

Also available from Open Chain:

The Busy Woman's Sewing Book
The Busy Woman's Fitting Book
both by Nancy Zieman with Robbie Fanning
each $12 postpaid ($12.65, California residents)
Learn Bearmaking
by Judi Maddigan
$18 postpaid ($19, California residents)

As a special service for Claire Shaeffer's fans, we sell all of her books that are in print:

The Complete Book of Sewing Shortcuts, $12.95.
Price It Right (for dressmakers), $4.
Sew A Beautiful Gift, $12.95.
Claire Shaeffer's Fabric Sewing Guide, April 1989, $24.95

Send orders to Open Chain at the address above. Add $2.00 postage for the first book plus 50 cents per additional book. California residents please add 7% tax (before shipping charges).

Meanwhile, hug your sewing machine.

Do you have a sewing question for Claire? Write her c/o Open Chain Publishing at the address above. Please keep your questions on a separate piece of paper from orders. Sorry, but questions cannot be individually answered.